Heal Yourself

of Sickness, Fear, Worry, Unhappiness,
and Hard Luck

Heal Yourself

of Sickness, Fear, Worry, Unhappiness,
and Hard Luck

C. & R. Anthony, Inc.
Publishers
New York

"A Master Publication"

FIRST EDITION

Copyright, 1940, by
ELLIOTT PUBLISHING CO., INC.

SECOND REVISED EDITION

Copyright, 1950, by
C. & R. Anthony, Inc.

15th Printing—Dec. 1960

MANUFACTURED IN THE UNITED STATES OF AMERICA

Contents

Introduction

FOR 25 years I tried to make my thinking help me to get rid of sickness, unhappiness, fear, worry and hard luck. For 25 years I spent endless hours of misery reading boresome books on how to make my thought heal me. For 25 years I tried to understand their big words and long, foggy sentences.

This tiresome toil moved me to take a vow. The vow was that I would try to get a clear understanding of how to make my thinking heal. Then I would give it to the sorrowing souls of this world in simple words. I hope I have been able to do so in these pages.

I did not write this book to please the tiny 2% of our people who went through college. I wrote it for the millions of sad hearts who hardly ever read a book, but who long to be healed of sickness, unhappiness, fear, worry and bad luck.

To them I give it without any money profit for myself. I have also withheld my name to shun personal praise if there should be any. For as Thoreau said, "What we do for money or fame isn't worth doing."

I do not claim that I myself can make these teachings do miracles of healing. If I could I would fade out of sight as Jesus did. You can probably make the teachings of this book do more for you than they have done for me. For pupils often outgrow their teacher.

You are not urged to agree with what I have set forth here. Believe it or doubt it. Take it or leave it, as you wish. I am not a healer. I take no patients. I am only a business man. Everything I have said in these pages about medicine and disease of the fleshly body has been OK'd by a doctor.

If we desire to make this book heal we will have to study it and not merely read it. The author himself finds it necessary to study it, for even he forgets its many healing thoughts.

I do not claim that I have given you all there is to know about the Truth. I have merely written here some of the things I have learned about truth during the last 45 years.

What I have told you has overcome sickness, unhappiness, fear, worry, and hard luck for me. I hope my experience will help or heal you. With badwill to none and Goodwill to all, I offer this book to suffering humanity which knows not why it suffers.

CHAPTER 1

Badwill vs. Goodwill Thinking

ALL through this book we mention badwill vs. Goodwill thinking.

By badwill thinking we mean: Hate, anger, irritation. Strife, strain, tension. Jealousy, revenge, vanity. Coveting, criticism. Cursing, cruelty. Fear, worry. Self-pity. Lying, stealing, cheating. Love of empty talk and amusements. Gloomy thoughts, discontent.

Love of rotten stories, adultery, lust after women. Love of being boss. Love of smoking and drinking. Love of flattery. Love of ease. Love of self and the bad in the world. Love of fame, money, power. No love for our Lord Jesus (God), and the good in our brothers.

These badwill thoughts are 34 infernal poisons that race into us from hell. They poison us with sickness, unhappiness, fear, worry and hard luck.

By Goodwill we mean love. Love of everything and everybody. Love of our Lord Jesus (God) and the good in our brothers. Goodwill-love-thoughts burn up the badwill thoughts. They burn up the 34 badwill poisons in us from hell and bring health, happiness and freedom from fear, worry, hard luck.

Thus whenever you see the word badwill in the following pages, it means the 34 poisonous thoughts in us from hell. And whenever you see the word Goodwill, it means love thoughts from heaven.

CHAPTER 2

What Man Is

OUR fleshly body is not man. It is merely a house given us to live in while we are here on earth. Inside of our fleshly body is our spiritual body.

Our spiritual body has the same organs in it that we have in our fleshly body. Has the same shape and look as our fleshly body. But our spiritual body is made out of spirit instead of flesh.

In both our spiritual and our fleshly body there is a starter like the starter in our automobile. It works in both bodies at the same time. It is called our *Will*. It starts everything we do. Also in our two bodies there is an engine like the engine in our car. This engine is our *Thinking*. Our *Will* starts our *Thinking*. Then our *Thinking* does what our *Will* tells us to.

Our two bodies have no power of their own. They do exactly what our *Will* and *Thinking* tell them to. If our *Will* and *Thinking* tell them to think *badwill* thoughts, they obey. And then our two bodies suffer from sickness, unhappiness, fear, worry or hard luck. If our *Will* and *Thinking* tell our bodies to think *Goodwill* thoughts, our bodies do so. Then our two bodies rejoice in health, happiness, freedom from fear, worry and hard luck.

The power that makes our *Will* and *our Thinking* do things does not come from us. It flows into our spiritual body and then into our fleshly body from our Lord Jesus (God). It floats in through *His Holy Spirit*.

When our fleshly body dies our *Will* and *Thinking* cast it off like an old, worn-out coat. Then our *Will* and our *Thinking* keep on working in our spiritual body. They live in it and work in it forever. For our *Will* and our *Thinking* are our deathless life given to us by our Lord Jesus (God). Our *Will* and our *Thinking* is our eternal soul. It never dies but lives on forever.

Please remember what our soul is for we shall use the word soul all through this book.

CHAPTER 3

Law of Come-Back

THERE are many fixed laws that run the universe. Such as the law of day and night. Birth and death. Spring, summer, winter and autumn. The law of gravity and the law of *Come-Back*.

The law of *Come-Back* brings back to us every thought we send out. Every thought we think goes out from us and comes back to us like an echo or boomerang. Sir Isaac Newton, the great scientist, told of this law. He said, "To every action there is an equal reaction."

If we send out thoughts of badwill they will come back to us and poison us with sickness, unhappiness, fear, worry and hard luck. If we send out thoughts of goodwill, they come back and bless us with health, happiness; also with freedom from fear, worry and bad luck.

We have to pay for every badwill thought with suffering of some kind. These thoughts always come back and poison us.

An old philosopher said, "Beware! Beware! Whatever proceeds from you will return to you." Jesus warned us of this law of *Come-Back* when He said, "Be not deceived; God is not mocked: for whatsoever a man soweth, that shall he also reap."

CHAPTER 4

Why I Was Sick

UP TO the age of 32 I was boiling over with health, pep and great driving power. I worked day and night and Sundays to build up my own business from a small start. I had neither money nor experience in the business I had chosen. All I had was a giant's strength to work and fight.

At 32 I went to pieces. Not only my throat and lungs were sick but also my stomach, heart, liver and kidneys. I sat up in a chair for 10 days at the point of death. For 7 weeks I was not out of danger.

However, I got well. The doctor said my animal strength carried me through. But I believe I was spared to pass through a bitter experience so as to write it in this book for the help of others who are suffering.

Yes, I got over my illness but it left me a wreck to fight through 19 years of nervous hell.

When I went back to work my business and I personally were deeply in debt. My business was on the edge of failure. Then I had a second breakdown. I was taken down with erysipelas which is a kind of blood poison. It seemed as if the whole world was against me.

The doctors did all they could. I return thanks for their unselfish help. But a friend suggested I try doctoring my thought instead of my body. I did. I went into it with all my heart just as I went into everything else. I spent two hours nearly every day in reading and in silent thought to purify my thinking.

For 19 long years I struggled faithfully to make my thought give me health, happiness and daily needs. It did help me. I am most thankful for the blessed relief it gave me and for the

5

help of the doctor of thought who worked with me. But in spite of his earnest work and mine I was not able to get rid of my nervous breakdown. It was my fault; not his or his teaching. I wasn't willing to let his teaching heal me.

At the end of 19 years of trying to make my thought cure my fleshly miseries I began to find it hard to breathe when I lay down in bed. I also suffered from dizziness during the day. This stirred up new haunting fears. For now I was sure that my nervousness had turned into heart trouble or some serious ailment of the body.

Then came the third breakdown. In the middle of the night at Watch Hill, Rhode Island, I awakened with greater breathing trouble than ever. Both arms were numb and there was a big lump in the pit of my stomach.

My doctor of thought told me to go to a doctor of the flesh and find out what I ought to eat. I had not been to a doctor of the flesh for 19 years. I was shivering with fear lest he should tell me I had heart trouble. I was lucky to find a cheerful osteopathic physician (a doctor who stirs up the flow of the blood by exercising muscles and nerves with his hands. The flow of blood fights disease without medicine).

He said I had gall bladder trouble, sluggish liver and unnatural decay of food in the bowels. But I would get over them if I would let him make my blood flow freely.

Having learned the power of thought over the flesh I couldn't sell myself on doctoring my flesh alone. I let the osteopath keep up his work because it made me feel better. But I knew that my ailments were coming from some wrong thought which must change or I would never get well.

Then this idea came to me: Everything is changing every minute. Our thoughts, our bodies, our styles, customs, habits —even the universe is forever changing. Therefore, why can't my thought about my sickness change to the thought of health? Why can't my thought of misery change to the thought of happiness? Why can't my thought of failure change to a thought of success? If everything else is changing "There is always a chance that my thought can change."

Nothing in my 19 years' study of healing ever filled me with such hope as THERE IS ALWAYS A CHANCE THAT THOUGHT CAN CHANGE. For I knew that if there really was a chance for my thought to change, my troubles would change. So I began a big drive to change my thinking.

I was full of the notion that I had been suffering from neurasthenia for 19 years. Neurasthenia means nervous weakness brought on by years of strained thinking and overwork. Also, since seeing the osteopath I thought I was suffering from gall bladder and liver trouble and from unnatural decay of food in the bowels.

But I was not suffering from these ailments at all. I found that I was suffering from badwill thinking. And I saw for the first time that the way out of my miseries of the flesh and business was to change my badwill thinking to Goodwill thinking. The help that this change of thought gave me was amazing, as we shall see in the next chapter.

CHAPTER 5

Good Nature

NOW I want to talk about one kind of badwill which was poisoning me without my knowing it. I want to talk about angry irritation. By irritation I mean going into an ill-natured rage every time something goes wrong.

For 43 years I have been the head of a business, always driving something or somebody, always trying to rule everybody and everything with my badwill.

The job of the head of a business is to make people and things work smoothly. But they won't, no matter what we do. Therefore 9 business drivers out of 10 are as I was—always in fits of irritation and anger because of the never-ending troubles that come up in business every day.

I never thought anything about this wrathful irritation until I learned what badwill is and how it works and what it was doing to me. I looked upon business as a fight and thought the head of a business had to fight to keep the works running right.

Therefore imagine my surprise when my second teacher told me what was making my nervous breakdown, breathing trouble, liver trouble, gall bladder trouble, unnatural decay of food in the bowels and some of my other ailments. And what was making them? That kind of badwill called high-strung, angry irritation!

No doctor ever told me anything about irritation. But now I had looked for the cause of my ailments and had found that my angry "blow-ups" over little things were making a large part of my fleshly misery.

I found out that irritation, anger and working or eating in a strain over-excite the adrenal glands. These glands are located on top of the kidneys. Dr. Boris Sokoloff, in the *American Weekly*, calls them the "mad" glands. He explains that when we need to brace ourselves for a fight these adrenal glands shut off digestion and flood our blood with a fighting chemical called adrenalin.

When the fight, irritation or anger is over, our muscles should quiet us down by oozing out a lazy acid called lactic acid into our blood. Our muscles do ooze this lazy, quieting acid into our blood if we are outdoors exercising like children or savages.

But when we of the indoor life get irritated, high-strung or angry, our indoor muscles don't pour out enough lazy lactic acid to quiet us down. Therefore the adrenalin, stirred up by our rage, keeps us all keyed up ready to fight much of the time.

This tightens up our nerves, stomach, bowels and other organs. Then we find ourselves sick with some kind of illness such as nervous jitters, nervous sweating, cold or hot feeling all over, neurosis, neurasthenia, headache, dizziness, gall bladder trouble, liver trouble, indigestion, constipation, ulcers of the stomach etc.

Therefore it was natural for the doctors to find that my stomach, gall bladder, liver and bowels were not working properly. They were all tightened up so that they could not work in their regular healthy way. But they might have doctored them for years without giving me much, if any, relief.

It remained for me to find out that angry irritation and working in strife and strain were forms of badwill that were hindering my organs from working healthily. And just as soon as I began to try and stop my bad, fighting, irritating thoughts I began to get relief.

But "believe you me" the stopping of these vicious thoughts was not easy. For I had cemented these badwill thoughts for 43 years into a habit of thinking as hard as cement.

However, I would remember "There is ALWAYS a chance that thought can change." No matter how stubborn my habits of irritation, anger and straining were, I would declare "They

CAN change." I would declare "It is all a matter of being willing to have them change."

So I started to say to myself on and off all day long, "I am willing to change my thoughts from irritation, anger, strife and strain to peacefulness, forgiveness, patience and good nature."

It didn't work so "hot" at first for I was not really willing to let my irritation change. I was only willing to repeat the words like a parrot. I was not willing to feel them. However, I finally did begin to mellow into a willingness to believe that I could change.

Then without realizing it, my change of thought began to do something to me. My digestion began to get better. The liver and gall bladder trouble and the gas from unnatural decay in the bowels began to go away. The hard breathing and nervousness began to go away. They all began to go away without my knowing it.

Naturally I didn't notice the change, for the old human animal seldom notices the good that is happening to him. He only sees his troubles. This is especially true of an irritated, angry, high-strung person like me. So I didn't realize that my digestion was getting better or that my nervousness and tightness were going away. But they were all stealing away as darkness steals away before the dawn. I had let in the light of Goodwill thinking and the night of badwill was passing away.

And down in my business office the mountains of troubles began to melt into harmony. The jobs I hated to do began to be a pleasure. The jobs that always were so hard became easy. The tangles that seemed hard to work out opened up and almost straightened out themselves.

And every one in my office began to be happier in his work. Moreover, business seemed to flow in from every direction. And my family which had suffered under my gloom so long began to call me "Happy Pappy."

But I would "fall off the wagon" many times during the day and let myself slide back into my old habits of irritation, anger and strife. I would slip back in the twinkling of an eye before I realized it because of the long years of habit. Then several days afterward my liver and gall bladder and bowels and nerves would begin to "blow up." Then I would wonder what I had eaten to cause all this trouble.

But I learned that what I had eaten had nothing to do with it. I was suffering from my irritation, anger and strain. I had sent these thoughts out and they were coming back to make me feel fierce. If my food was not digesting properly it was my thinking and not the food that was causing my indigestion.

I would take a pencil and write down all of the irritations and angry fits and strains I had fallen into for several days back. I was surprised at the number of them. Then I would see that they and not my food were the cause of my fleshly suffering.

This was a very hard thing for me to get through my head. For all my life I had thought that every ailment of the flesh came from the flesh. The doctors had taught me this. So had my parents. I was raised on it. Therefore it was no little task for me to trace my suffering back to my badwill thinking.

And let me repeat that the suffering from these black thoughts would not show up on my body for several days after they had happened. It seemed to take several days for the echoes of irritation to come back.

"How am I ever going to stop these irritations?" I would say to myself. Then I saw the way. I saw that whenever I got irritated or mad or under strife and strain, I and no one else had to suffer. I saw that I had to pay the price for my irritation. So I asked myself, "Is it worth it?"

I saw that every time I sent out a thought of irritation or anger or strain it was going to come right back to me and make me suffer. When I got this into my head I began to change to calmness, forgiveness, patience and good nature. I learned that no amount of money could pay me for having even one small irritation.

After I had gotten pretty well trained in good nature I found I could tell when I was getting under badwill during a business day. I would get nervous or feel a lump in the pit of my stomach. But I learned how to snap out of it. I sat down and thought a good thought for somebody who I knew was in trouble or suffering. I found this a wonderful way to soften my hard, bad nature into good nature.

After I had overcome much of my irritation, anger and strain I found myself going about every job during the day with peace, calmness and ease. If I was trying to catch a train I found myself allowing more time than was necessary. I would arrive at the railroad station ten minutes ahead of time. This stopped irritation and strain.

If I missed a train I would say, "I'm glad of the delay because it makes me let down and loosen up." I would say to myself, "I make delays to stop all strife and strain." If I had to go to a meeting I allowed so much time that I could walk to it carefree with no tight feeling in the pit of my stomach.

If I had a hard piece of work to do I found myself going at it not as a hardship but rather as an interesting job. Then the trouble in the job began to melt away. I found all of my work changing to a peaceful, pleasing pastime instead of an explosion of irritation, anger, strife and badwill fighting.

For 20 years I had played golf always in a strain and rush. I used to ride 20 miles from my home to my office on Saturdays. I spent half a day there in business strife. Then I grabbed a sandwich and a glass of milk and rushed back 20 miles to the golf course.

There I would tear through the changing of my clothes and dash out to the first tee and fret because of the delay in getting started. Then I would fume because the foursome ahead held us up. I would fret over lost balls and fly into anger at every bad shot I made, never giving thanks for good ones. Also we would make a lot of bets. All this put strain on my digestive organs for 3 hours until the game was over.

So I began to play golf alone or with some soul of happy heart who enjoyed playing leisurely. And I would never play except when I had plenty of time and my thought was loose and happy. Also if I got tired I would not play the full 18 holes, for I learned that the playing of a fixed 18 holes may overdo one's strength and make one feel worse than no golf at all. And as for playing 36 holes, that is committing slow suicide!

You can never believe the difference in my feelings and restful sleep after playing relaxed golf. And as for my score, it went down from the nineties to as low as 74. What nonsense to think we can play good golf in a strain! No athletics can be played successfully unless we are loose, free, calm and joyous.

Later on I stopped playing golf altogether. Instead, I now take long, peaceful walks in the country where I can relax and love the flowers and trees and streams and nature. As soon as I stopped golf and got my exercise from happy, relaxed walking I got rid of a sour stomach which gave me no end of suffering every summer during the golf season. Also I began to feel much better when I got away from all that golf strain and irritation.

I used to take a walk of 40 minutes from my office to the ferry on my way home every night. I did not allow myself a full 40 minutes, so I had to walk fast in a strain to catch the ferry. I never could figure out why this walk did me so little good. Sometimes it did me harm—made me shaky, nervous and upset my stomach. Also my sleep afterward was full of dreams of strife.

Then I learned to take a whole hour for this walk. I walked leisurely, looking in windows and strolling along all loose and free. When I arrived home from these relaxed walks I was glowing with a delicious, peaceful, let-down feeling and my sleep lost a large part of its dreams of strife.

It is a question in my mind whether relaxation and rest are not more important to a strained business man than exercise. It depends on our age and how easily our nerves are upset. If we can't sit still and enjoy a book or the peace of doing nothing, we should stop exercise or cut it down and rest. If we suffer from this kind of strung-up feeling we should learn to stay in bed over a whole weekend and read and sleep and rest. And what's more, we should learn to enjoy it.

What "dumb eggs" we mortals be! We know not what we do that makes our thoughts and bodies and lives a human hell.

We think a vacation is a builder of fleshly strength. But a vacation is merely letting our thinking take a rest from our daily badwill strife.

At this writing I am not entirely out of irritation but I am on the way and am deeply thankful for the harmony which the overcoming of irritation has brought to my health, happiness and business. I was always irritated, as Dr. Carrel says, and didn't know it.

But I am finding that irritation, anger and strife come in two kinds: the kind which explodes and the kind we don't notice. I have been able to overcome most of the bad nature which explodes. But I find that underneath there are countless small irritating thoughts which work in secret.

Here are some of them: Can't make the telephone work! Can't find a letter on my desk! Stenographer made a fool error! Can't rely on anyone to do anything but myself! Traffic lights always against me! Rotten drivers everywhere! Safety razor blades no good! Always a caller at office whom we don't want to see! Somebody trying to take advantage of us! Servants doing something dumb! The toast WOULD fall to the floor on the buttered side!

Don't we have these irritations happen to us all day long? But we've got to take them good-naturedly or pay the price in suffering. Charles Schwab said, "When things seem to be the worst just laugh at them." Mr Schwab was right. The best way to overcome an irritation is to laugh at it. It is just as easy to laugh at things which irritate us as it is to get mad at them. Getting irritated at something that goes wrong is a habit which we have built up without knowing it. We can build up a habit of laughing at them if we want to. And how this laughing at them does cut the poison out of irritation and change us over to the healing power of good nature! Good nature is a wonderful healer. That is why good-natured people are nearly always healthy and live so long.

We can have a lot of fun out of irritation if we laugh at it, for irritations are silly and we can see the funny side of them if we try to.

Medical science is just beginning to understand that badwill, such as irritation, hate, anger, etc., causes disease. Bad nature poisons the body; good nature heals it and makes it happy and successful.

An osteopathic doctor told me about one of his patients who had an awful temper. One day the doctor had a date to play golf with him. The doctor arrived at the club a little late.

The patient stormed and raged in fierce anger. The doctor told me he knew the patient would come to his office in a day or so to be doctored for stiff muscles. Sure enough, he came to the doctor 3 days after the fit of anger with his back all stiff and bent over!

The doctor told me that this patient had carried on this way for years with fits of anger followed by stiff muscles, lame back and general bad feeling all over the body. The doctor said, "This is just one of many cases I have which prove that irritation, anger and strain poison the body."

We put up with a lot of small, poisonous irritations that we could stop so easily. For example: I knew a woman who suffered most of her life from daily irritations caused by the lid of her coffee pot falling off. Finally she got sense enough to spend a few dollars for a new pot. I used a broken shaving brush for 15 years until I got sense enough to buy a new one. Think of 15 years of poisonous irritation about a shaving brush!

We had an electric light hanging from the ceiling in our kitchen. For 20 years we groped angrily in the dark every night to find the string to that light. One day somebody suggested that for $3. we could put in a switch with a wall button. Twenty years of poison which could have been kept out of our bodies for $3!

Carrying a load of badwill such as irritation, fear, worry, hate, anger, etc., is a terrible dead weight to pack around with us while trying to make a success. I carried it most of my life and had to succeed in spite of it. Think what I could have done if I had dumped out this heavy burden and let the power of Goodwill carry me through life's work in a good-natured mood!

The president of a certain great chain of stores has a giant business load to carry but he never gets angry. An article in *Fortune Magazine* says that he spends his days wandering through his offices, talking pleasantly and good-naturedly with his men.

What a lot of poison he keeps out of his body by keeping away from irritation, anger, strife and bad nature! His face tells of the peace that glows inside of him. And let it be noted that his good nature shines in his well-managed stores. For as the head of a business, so the business.

A man full of irritation and other kinds of badwill shows it in his hard face, hard voice, hard thought and in the lines of his hands. Thus it is proven that as our thought, so our body. We should "watch and pray" that we don't get pickled in irritation and badwill with a heart as hard as stone.

The storm door on my back porch got to sticking on account of damp weather. I was fighting it angrily every time I opened it. The irritation I exploded was fierce. One day I got hold of myself and found that a gentle, quiet push of the toe of my shoe opened it easily without any irritating poison. How many foolish shots of poison we send into ourselves by such nonsense!

Barking dogs used to stir me but one day a lover of dogs said, "I never hear any dogs barking." He loved dogs so their barking was music to him. After I got that point of view dogbarking irritated me very little. In like manner many people get irritated at roosters crowing and report it to the police. But rooster crowing never stirred any angry irritation in me because I like roosters and love to hear them crow at the break of day.

I was in a rage one night about the noise of a street carnival in our town. My teacher said, "They are having a good time. Don't you want them to enjoy themselves? Stop thinking of yourself and think of their happiness." That stopped my lifelong irritation about such things.

Motor-car drivers have a bad habit of getting irritated and angry at other drivers. What a lot of poison that fills us with! Let's love the other driver and forgive him if he makes a mistake, for we make just as many mistakes as other drivers. "Every man has need to be forgiven" and in forgiving him we fill our bodies with healing instead of poison.

I wonder if we ever stop to realize that our criticism of others is only the seeing of our own faults in the other fellow.

Dr. Fosdick says that the curse of our modern business life is doing everything in a hurry. We must make money quick. We must do everything quick. This straining to get everything done quick fills us with irritation, anger and bad nature. For in most cases we can't get things done quickly and then we blow up.

Some wise man said, "It takes a certain amount of time to do everything." What a lot of irritation we would save ourselves if we followed that rule in our daily life! We would not only do away with irritation but would get our work done quicker and better. For as Benjamin Franklin said, "Haste makes waste."

Will Rogers was a marvelous example of good nature. He said, "I never saw a man I didn't like." What a beautiful, healing thought! All that loving good nature he sent out came back and blessed him with a wonderfully happy life.

Except for the foolish chance he took in the Alaska plane he would have lived to great age for he was so free from the poison of irritation, anger and bad nature! Will Rogers boiled inside with love and good nature which came back to him and gave him health, happiness and wealth.

"An angry man is always wrong and full of poison," said a wise old Chinaman. We laugh at the Chinese as a backward race. But we don't understand them. They know far more than we do about many things. They know how to live and we don't. They know from 4 thousand years of experience that bad nature brings back poison, unhappiness and failure. They know that the rarest jewels of life are patience, good nature and peace.

Their music is full of good nature. So is the sound of their voice and language. So are their manners and customs. When invaders sent armies to conquer them many years ago they said, "We hope we will soon find out whom we belong to so we can return to our regular life of peace and happiness."

What a healing thought this is! How different from the irritation, hate, anger and revenge that would have belched out in resentment from us of the West! We would have flooded our bodies with badwill poison in fighting back. But the wise and experienced Chinese would rather have health and happiness than poison their bodies to please their pride.

The Chinese by nature cannot fight back at an enemy after the manner of modern Western ideas. They can't do it. For their long experience as a race knows that irritation, anger and war are poison to the body. They know that humility brings peace of mind. True, they are fighting now but against their will.

When the Allies beat the Germans in World War I they satisfied their irritation, hate, anger, greed and pride by taking their full "pound of flesh" from the Germans at Versailles.

The Chinese looked on and smiled. Their policy is never to take more than half of an advantage gained over an enemy. This, they claim, makes friends of the enemy and keeps off another war. Wonderful wisdom that, for witness World War II which was Germany's revenge for the Treaty of Versailles!

Lin Yutang in his charming book THE IMPORTANCE OF LIVING says that the 3 great weaknesses in American life are hope for wealth, doing things perfectly and being on time. He also says that the Chinese nation has always been more wise and easy-going than perfect. If it had tried to be as perfect as we of the West he says it could never have lived its long life of 4 thousand years. For he says that 4 thousand years of perfect living would drain the life out of any nation.

An important outcome of being wise and easy-going instead of perfect, he says, is the scarcity of insanity in China. In the West, he says, the insane are so many that they are put in asylums, while in China the insane are so few that the Chinese worship them.

Think of it! Before the present Communist Government, there were hardly any insane among 450,000,000 Chinese where they live a life of peace and sweetness and serenity. Whereas our Western life of irritation, anger and high-strung work fills our insane asylums with ever-increasing numbers of broken, nervous wrecks. If I had not learned the poison of irritation, anger and strain I would have died of insanity or disease of the liver, gall bladder and bowels.

Verily, verily, irritation, anger, bad nature and other kinds of badwill thinking flood us with the poison of ill health, fear, unhappiness and failure! We should not get mad at anyone or anything. If we do we will suffer. The Law of *Come-back* will echo the anger back to us and it will show up in some sort of disease, unhappiness, fear or business loss.

Here is a nice thought to begin the day with: "When you awaken in the morning think and say to yourself and chant it, 'Child of Light, go forth into your day, striving to render gentle service to all that lives, knowing that you are a brother to all that lives.'

"Knowing that you are brother to all that lives, you will know that you speak harshly to yourself if you speak harshly to another. You hurt yourself if you are unkind to a dog or a cat or step carelessly on a little worm. You hurt yourself when you kick a stone in anger—for the stone is a brother life." What blesses one, blesses all. What curses one, curses all.

I heard that John D. Rockefeller, Senior, used to lean over to anyone bawling him out, with his hand behind his ear. He did it good-naturedly. He never got mad or excited. He was too smart to poison himself with irritation, anger and strife. He was always calm, even in the most trying cases. This is doubtless one of the reasons for his success and long life.

We who get mad like to get mad. That's why we do it.

Jesus knew the poison of badwill and used Goodwill instead because he knew it paid. Straining at our work is a kind of irritation and anger. It is badwill. The law of *Come-Back* always brings it back and makes us suffer with disease, sleeplessness, misery or business failure.

Even if we win temporary business success by strife and strain we will find ourselves sunk in ill health, sorrow, remorse, unhappiness, fear or something bad, for no good thing can come out of badwill.

A New York *Times* editorial said that the "peaceful, inward

life of John Wesley enabled him to live 88 happy and triumphant years though making 40 thousand addresses and fighting
numberless outside strains."

When we get irritated or angry we blame it on something
that happened outside of us. But we made that something happen by our irritated, angry, striving, straining thoughts. Nothing outside of us made it happen. When our heart is full of
calmness, forgiveness, patience and good nature nothing bobs
up to make us irritated or angry.

We who suffer from strife and strain should read THE
PRACTICE OF THE PRESENCE OF GOD by Brother Lawrence. You will find it in the back of this book.

The story of his calm, peaceful life soothes and quiets irritation in a marvelous way.

Whenever I "get up in the air" from the strain of irritation,
anger, overdoing or overthinking or talking too much, I say to
myself, "Now, old boy, get hold of yourself. You've got to be
willing to settle down and be quiet, peaceful and serene inside.
You've got to sit right down and get sweet inside and think
of *nothing* for a solid hour." If I am really willing to do so I
come right down to earth and all is well.

Pray to our Lord Jesus (God) to help you love Him and
your brothers instead of loving yourself. That will overcome
irritation. For love of self-comfort is the main cause of irritation. Pray the Lord to help you "grow backwards to the innocence and gentleness of childhood."

Down on the street where I live there are hardly any husbands left—only widows. The husbands were all heads of large
business companies. They were all business drivers. They killed
themselves with badwill fighting for money. True, they left
their widows a comfortable income but killed themselves in
doing it. What a pity that the teachings of this chapter were
not known to them!

Look at the big politicians and business men who have
cracked up under strife and strain, irritation and anger. To
name a few, I would mention Mayor LaGuardia of New York,
all our Secretaries of State for years back, the president of the

great First National Bank in New York, James Forrestal, Secretary of Defense, President Roosevelt.

I pray that this book may reach and heal all business drivers, as well as all other people who are suffering from the habit of irritation, anger, strife, strain and other kinds of badwill. We can change. We don't have to be that way. If we are willing we can all change from bad nature to good nature, from badwill thinking to Goodwill thinking, and reap its blessed gift of health, happiness, fearlessness and success.

CHAPTER 6

Prayer and Healing

PRAYER will always bring a healing if we are out of debt to the law of COME-BACK. But if our suffering has not paid off our debt to the law of COME-BACK for our badwill thinking, no prayers may heal us.

For to heal us in spite of the law of COME-BACK God would have to break this law. God cannot break any of His laws for running the universe. If He changed the slightest thing in His program whereby He runs everything from worlds to fleas, we would have a cataclysmic catastrophe.

When we want a healing or answer to prayer it is we who must change. We must pay off our debts to the law of COME-BACK by suffering and change to goodwill thinking.

My son was healed of TB seemingly by a Christian Science practitioner. My first teacher was seemingly healed of terrible rheumatism. And Dr. Alexis Carrel saw a man's hand healed of cancer right before his eyes at the Shrine of Lourdes.

But I believe that these healings came to pass because the patients had paid off their debts to the law of COME-BACK. They had suffered out of their debts to the law of COME-BACK. They had struck a balance with the law of COME-BACK just at the time of their healings. That's why they were healed. My son was young and therefore had little badwill thinking chalked up against him.

We are all "born in sin and brought forth in iniquity." This means that we were born with a liking for badwill thoughts. We got this love of these hell thoughts from our ancestors all the way back to Adam.

We have 34 badwill thoughts born into us. They include hate, anger, and irritation as we said in the second chapter.

These 34 dense clouds of poisonous badwill thinking, hovering around our heart, keep us from getting a healing. Because the Holy Spirit of our Lord Jesus, which lives in our heart, cannot break through these black clouds of poison and heal us.

Therefore to get a healing we must pay off our debts to COME-BACK by suffering and try to wipe these 34 poisons out of our heart. This is not easy to do, for they were born in us. We can't get rid of them ourselves. We have to pray to our Lord Jesus for help. He will help us—help us wonderfully— if we sincerely try to get rid of these badwill thoughts and pray to Him for help.

The beautiful author of THE GOLDEN FOUNTAIN says that if we try to destroy the 34 poisons and pray to Jesus for help, He will carry us all the way to freedom from them and into a holy, heavenly heart. And no sickness, fear, worry, unhappiness or hard luck can live in a heart free from the 34 badwill thoughts which are all poison.

Healing comes from prayer—prayer for a pure heart. But I never knew how to pray until I learned something about it from my saintly friend in Boston and from the writings of Emanuel Swedenborg. Here is what I learned about praying. Much of this is taken from our essays entitled WHY OUR PRAYERS ARE NOT ANSWERED and WHY WE DON'T GET A HEALING.

1. We should try hard to chase the 34 poisons out of our heart and pray to our Lord Jesus to help us.

2. Don't pray on Sunday only or once in a while or once a day. We should pray all the time we can. "Pray without ceasing," as the Bible says.

3. If we seem to get no answer, just keep on praying as Sadhu Sundar Singh did. He prayed for 2 years without any sign of an answer. But he never gave up. Finally Jesus appeared in his room. From then on his spirit was taken up into heaven about 8 times a month.

4. Most of us never pray unless we want something to make

us happy and comfortable. Our Lord Jesus (God) will not answer selfish "gimme" prayers. He will never, never help us to be selfish.

When we are in pain or trouble we can pray for whatever we seem to need. But we should finish our prayers as Jesus did: "Father, if it be possible, let this cup pass from me: nevertheless not as I will, but as thou wilt." Then let us be satisfied with whatever happens for it is for our best good.

5. At least half of our prayers should be prayers of praise and thanksgiving. We should give thanks for our many blessings. Name each of them. Sing songs of praise and thanksgiving to Him (Jesus) all day. Sing in words or sing in words and music.

6. Most of us don't have our heart in our prayers. Our prayers are just wooden words. Often many of them are cold, hollow words, long-drawn-out. We don't love to pray. We don't love our Lord Jesus (God). Therefore how can we love to pray to Him?

How can we make a success out of what we don't love to do? No, we don't love our Lord Jesus and the good in our brothers. We love the 34 poisons. If we try to love our Lord and the 34 poisons at the same time, there is no use praying.

For we are plain sinners and we know that our Lord Jesus (God) "heareth not sinners: but if any man be a worshipper of God, and doeth his will, him he heareth."

It is not flowery words and long prayers that get an answer. It is our deep love for our Lord Jesus and love of the good in our brothers that reaches Jesus. That tender love for Him makes His boundless love for us come back to us and give us an answer. His love for us is so tender and deep that He would rather suffer a thousand crucifixions than see us suffer one second.

Love is the wave length that carries our prayers to Him. If we have little love for Him and the good in our brothers, we are off the wave length that carries prayer to our Lord. We are tuned out of Station J-E-S-U-S and are praying to a dead "mike." We are praying to Satan instead of Jesus.

7. We put on a manner of "sackcloth and ashes" when we pray. We think we have to kneel down on a hard floor and look sad like we do at a funeral or in church. We don't have to kneel. We can pray sitting, standing, walking or lying down. And instead of looking sour we should be joyous with praise. Also happy with love for our Lord Jesus and the good in our brothers. Jesus wants us to make pleasure, not hardship, out of prayer.

8. Many of us have a set speech which we make in our prayers. We grind through the same words and thoughts in each prayer. This is especially so when we pray out of prayerbooks. That's making a praying machine out of ourselves.

Instead of this machine praying we should pour out real, genuine love from the depths of our heart for our Lord Jesus. Say whatever comes into our heart. He will lead our heart to say the right things. Just talk with Jesus like we would with a brother in the room.

9. We really don't believe our prayers will be answered. We have no faith. After a long prayer I have often thought to myself, "Will it do any good?" How can we hope to get an answer when we feel like that?

Even when I get an answer to prayer my feeble faith wonders if the healing really came from prayer. Evil spirits argue to me that something else did the healing. Prayer without faith is like an automobile without gas. Goes nowhere.

Yes, devils will keep on filling us with doubts as long as we have the 34 poisons in us. For evil spirits ride into our hearts on these poisonous thoughts and argue that we should not have faith. When we delight in the 34 poisons we are connected by long distance wire with hell. Over this wire all the poisons of hell talk to us and shake our faith. Lack of faith is nothing but evil spirits in hell telling us to have no faith.

I have always thought faith was something we had to force on ourselves. But I have found that the way to get faith is to get a clear understanding of the Truth. For when we understand the Truth we can't help but believe in it. And I learned that the way to get a clear understanding of the Truth is to read THE TRUE CHRISTIAN RELIGION by Emanuel Swedenborg. Next to the Bible this is the greatest book ever written on religion.

Also when we get enough love for our Lord Jesus and the good in our brothers, the tender love of our Lord will glow us full of faith.

10. We don't sink ourselves down into a meek, lowly, humble surrender to the will of our Lord Jesus (God). Prayer is a mighty giving up and full surrender to His Will, knowing that His Will is always good.

11. We are bashful about praying. Too shy to even say grace before a meal. And if called upon to pray aloud in public or in a group we'd faint. We are ashamed of our most devoted friend and lover—the greatest man who ever walked on earth—our Lord Jesus. Like Peter, we are ashamed to admit that we are one of His disciples.

I have to overcome that feeling. But how can we get an answer to prayer when we are ashamed of it? Let the world laugh in its ignorance and darkness. While we, in His Light and Love, know that the honor of all honors is to be a pure, true disciple of Jesus—a comrade of our Lord Jesus (God).

Yes, Jesus said, "Go into thy closet and shut the door," but that doesn't mean we should be ashamed of praying. It means shut out the 34 poisons so our Lord Jesus can shine out of our heart and answer our prayers. But we must not be full of spiritual pride like the publican who loved to make long prayers in public and be heard of men.

We pray because we are afraid of God (our Lord Jesus). Afraid He will punish us for our sins. Such prayer tries to free us from the torment of fear. Therefore it is pure selfishness. God never answers any prayer that seeks to gratify a selfish desire.

Besides, God doesn't punish us for our sins. For God (our Lord Jesus) is Love. He knows nothing but Love and gives us nothing but Love. Our sins (the 34 poisons) are what punish us. The only way we can flee the torture that comes from the 34 poisons is to try to get rid of them. And pray to Him to help us overcome them.

13. We pray long and earnestly, thinking by long-winded wailing we will deserve a blessing. We can never earn an answer to prayer by words, no matter how many we pour out. And no matter how urgent and loud they are.

For such prayers are only a lot of ice-cold thoughts and noise trying to get something for our precious self. We don't want to give up the 34 poisons and surrender our whole heart to our Lord Jesus. So we detour around Him and try to earn an answer to prayer by much begging, beseeching and moaning.

14. Pray for our brothers as well as ourselves. Whatever we ask for ourselves we must ask it also for our brothers. This helps to take the selfishness out of our prayers.

15. The Lord's Prayer is the prayer of prayers. It is the most heavenly prayer ever uttered. It covers every human need. Every prayer should have the Lord's Prayer in it.

Also reading the Bible is wonderful prayer. For the Bible is the Voice and Word of God talking to us. Read the Bible and Swedenborg's books, for they show the hidden, spiritual meaning of the Bible. Read them as directed in the last chapter of this book entitled "What To Read For The Truth About Religion."

16. Go into silence for 15 minutes once a day or oftener. Chase all thoughts out of your mind and let Jesus talk to you silently. Stop talking to Him and let Him flow His Light and Love and Holy Spirit into your mind. The sweet, peaceful serenity that steals softly into our mind from this silence is amazing. So quieting, soothing, healing. But we must free our mind from every thought of self and the world and fully surrender our whole heart and mind to Him in silence.

17. We pray to the unreachable God instead of praying to our Lord Jesus. God is a man like we are. For we are made in His image and likeness. But the power of His thinking is far beyond our peewee thoughts.

His thinking knows no beginning or end. Swings out to the uttermost parts of the universe. Creates and runs the billions of suns and planets. Is without length, breadth, height, time, place or bounds. How can His gigantic thoughts bow down and listen to our little puny prayers? That would be like the

President of General Motors giving his time to the duties of the office boy.

Besides, God is pure Spirit and we are flesh. Flesh cannot mix with Spirit like oil can't mix with water. He can't understand our fleshly words and our fleshly brain can't understand His spiritual words. This is proven by the fact that when we go into our next life we have to speak a new tongue—the language of Spirit.

Furthermore, the lightning speed of His thinking is too fast for ours. Therefore any slow thinking prayer we offer up to Him is blown away by the rush of His thoughts like an ant in a hurricane. Again, His Light blazes with a brilliance that would blind us. How can our prayers reach Him through His blinding Light?

Moreover, think of the heat of our sun. If we could touch it, we'd burn up like a match in a volcano. Then think of the sun in heaven in which God lives.

It glows with the heat of Divine Love which even the highest angels can't bear. What becomes of our prayers offered direct to God which must go through the heat of the sun of heaven to get to Him? They of course melt and run away like hot lava before reaching Him.

When the spirit of Sadhu Sundar Singh was taken up into heaven he asked the angels, "Where is God?" They said, "God is boundless. We cannot see Him." Emanuel Swedenborg's spirit was taken up into heaven thousands of times. The angels told him many times that God is not reachable. God Himself told us we could not come near Him with our prayers when He said, "No man shall see my face and live."

How silly to pray to all that wide-spread Mind of pure Spirit! Doing so is like asking the United States for something. If we want something from the United States, we don't ask the United States for it. We ask the President of the United States. For he is the fleshly person through whom we reach the United States.

In like manner when we want to ask the great, vast Spirit of God for something, we should ask our Lord Jesus, who is

God in the flesh. For God had His size, mental motion, light and heat brought down to our level of thinking in the body of our Lord Jesus.

This gave us a fleshly person to pray to. A person like ourselves, who can hear our prayers and answer them like a loving brother would. Yet Jesus is God—God in the flesh. "I and my Father are one."

Suppose we want heat and light from our sun. Do we go direct to the sun for it? No! Because we can't reach the sun. And if we could it would put our eyes out and burn us up. So when we desire light and heat from our sun, we get in touch with our sun through its rays. For they are softened down to our weak way of receiving light and heat.

God in the fleshly body of Jesus stayed with us here on earth for 33 years. During that time He told us and showed us plainly that we should pray to our Lord Jesus (God in the flesh). He said clearly, "He that seeth ME seeth the Father."

He tried to make it easy for us by giving us God in the flesh to pray to. Then after Jesus ascended He left His Holy Spirit (God) in your heart and mine for us to pray to. He called it the Comforter. I always pray to "Our Father, Dear Lord Jesus, which art in the heavens and which art in the hearts of all my brothers and sisters, including myself."

Jesus told us many times in the Bible that we should only pray to Him. For example: "I am the way, the truth and the life. No man cometh unto the Father but by me." "He that tries to enter the sheepfold through some other door is a thief and a liar."

Yet some of us have prayed direct to the unreachable God for 2,000 years. Some of us say, "In the name of His Son, Jesus Christ," or "For the sake of His Son." This is worse still, because it makes two persons out of God, when the Father, the Son and the Holy Spirit are all One Person—God. Wonderful light on this can be had by reading THE TRUE CHRISTIAN RELIGION by Swedenborg.

The Old Testament tells how they talked with God direct and prayed to Him direct. But those who knew how to pray properly in those days prayed to Jehovah God. For Jehovah God of the Old Testament is the Lord Jesus Christ of the New Testament. Now we today know Jehovah God as Jesus.

The Holy Spirit of our Beloved Lord Jesus glows always in your heart, my heart and in every heart. His beautiful, loving Spirit ever longs to come out of our heart and answer our prayers and give us what we ought to have. For He said, "Behold, I stand at the door (of your heart) and knock. If any man hear my voice and open the door, I will come in unto him and will sup with him and he with Me."

But we don't "open the door" by praying to our beloved Lord Jesus. We pray to God whom no man can come near and live.

George Mueller of Bristol, England, raised $7,500,000. for his orphan home and other religious work. He never asked anyone for one cent. His prayers brought people to him bearing gifts. He prayed and waited. He often waited two years. But the answers always came. Never failed. He was no saint. Just a plain man like you and me. What he did, we can do, for "God is no respecter of persons." Read the book "George Mueller of Bristol."

When General Eisenhower was a boy, he got gangrene in his leg. The doctor wanted to cut it off. He would not consent. He suffered terrible agony. His family prayed in relays. They never gave up praying, although it seemed hopeless. They prayed day and night without ceasing. The leg was finally healed. The prayer of faith is *always* answered.

Try to love nothing but your beloved Lord Jesus and the good in your brothers. Try to lose all love for self and the world. Pray for love—love—ever more love. For love conquers everything. "Love never faileth."

If our prayers don't seem to be answered, just keep on trying to wipe out the 34 poisons. Keep on asking Jesus to help you overcome the poisons. Just keep on loving and praying. When we are free enough from the 34 poisons and our heart is full of love, our prayers will be answered and we will be healed here or in our next life. After death we will live in our beautiful, healthy, spiritual body. It looks exactly like our fleshly body but never grows over 30 years old.

And what's more glorious than any healing of the flesh, we will be taken straight up into heaven when we die. And there gain the only prize worth gaining in life—namely, the divine gift of being an angel.

CHAPTER 7

Healing Thoughts That Have Helped Me

WHEN Amelia Earhart flew the Atlantic she was told by old air men that she would "see" land before reaching it. They said, "You will 'see' it because you are so anxious to see it." And sure enough, she did "see" land several times before reaching and seeing the shore of Ireland.

A famous French aviator and his mechanic crashed in the desert. They were lost without water for 24 hours. Their fear and thirst were terrible. They "saw" caravans, searching parties, a lake of water, men with lights, etc., coming to save them. But none of these things were real. They were just unreal pictures of what they were so anxious to see.

In like manner we see disease, unhappiness, fear and failure because we are anxious to see them. "Oh no," we say. "I am not anxious to see them. I don't want them." But we do like to be sick, unhappy, afraid and in want. We don't know that we like them but we do. We like to grunt and complain about them and get others to sympathize with our misery.

We are unwilling to see health, happiness, fearlessness and success. We don't know that we are unwilling but we are. Thus being unwilling we do not bring harmony into our lives. We bring into our life just what we are willing to—just what we are willing to "see."

That many of us like to be sick is proven by this story told by a young doctor. He said, "I had just come out of medical school and hung up my doctor's sign. My first patient came in. He said, 'I feel fierce, Doc; I have fever. I am going to be a very sick man.'"

32

The young doctor looked him over thoroughly and found nothing wrong with him except that he needed a big dose of castor oil to clean out his bowels. The young doctor told him so. The man got mad, paid the young doctor's fee of $2. and left, slamming the door behind him with a bang.

The young doctor was dumbfounded. He couldn't understand why his good advice made the patient mad. He looked out of the window and saw the patient going into the office of an old doctor across the street. A week later the young doctor asked the old doctor how he treated this man.

The old doctor said, "I told him he was right in thinking he was a very sick man and that he had just come in time. I gave him some laxative pills and told him to go home and go to bed and I would call at his home at 3 o'clock. I saw him for several days until the laxative pills worked the junk out of his bowels. Then he was OK and willingly paid my bill of $30."

The young doctor said to the old doctor, "There wasn't anything the matter with that fellow except constipation. Why did he get mad at me and turn down my advice?"

The old doctor said, "You must learn that some people want to be sick. They won't be satisfied unless you agree with them and go through a lot of motions to nurse them out of their 'awful illness.' "

We can see the badwill or Goodwill thinking of a man in his face and eyes. Emerson said that the hard thoughts of a criminal are engraved in deep lines on his face. In like manner the Goodwill thinking of a child or a saintly person brightens their face with kindness and love.

Here are a few more lines from MAN THE UNKNOWN by Dr. Alexis Carrel. They clinched my faith in the fact that poisonous badwill thinking is the cause of ALL disease.

Dr. Carrel says that a regular habit of envy, hate and fear can start diseases. That business men who do not know how to fight worry die young and that highly excited feelings can harm our blood circulation. He points out that pleasure causes the skin of the face to flush, while fear turns it white.

He says it has been proved that a shock may cause marked

changes in the blood. Thought can injure our organs. The uncertainty of modern life, the endless nagging of it brings about diseases of stomach, bowels and indigestion.

He says that various kidney and bladder diseases can come in a round-about way from the poison of badwill thinking. Such diseases are almost unknown in countries where life is simpler and anxiety less. Likewise he says that those who keep peace glowing inside of them in the midst of high excitement are free from diseases of the nerves and organs.

I know a nervous, high-strung man. Whenever he gets excited over anything, even over a simple thing like taking a trip, he will get constipated and may not have a movement for 3 days and then only by the use of a laxative. Constipation is largely due to tight thinking which tightens up the bowels. Doesn't this show what our thinking does to our body?

What makes us change a walk into a run? What makes us bend over or stand up straight? What makes us go backward or forward? What makes us stick out our tongue or draw it in? What makes us frown or smile? Thinking—not flesh. In the same way, thinking—not flesh—makes our organs work sickly or healthily—makes us miserable or happy—makes us fail or succeed.

A doctor told me that when he was studying cancer of the stomach in medical school the teachings about cancer frightened him so that he could actually feel a cancer coming into his stomach. One of his classmates got so scared that he had a doctor examine him.

One of the greatest special cancer doctors in New York died of cancer. Also one of the greatest special lung doctors in New York died of consumption. He saved my life when I was at the point of death with diseased lungs. These cases show how our thoughts work on our flesh.

The King James translation of the Bible says, "It is the spirit that quickeneth; the flesh profiteth nothing." Lamsa's translation of these lines reads, "It is the spirit that giveth life. The body is of no account," which means that our soul (will and thinking) is life and the body merely clothes it.

Seagulls, polar bears, whales and thousands of other animals and birds were never educated about the weather nor taught that the ice is cold. Therefore they like cold water and cold weather and cold winds. But we human beings of the "high," scientific, fleshly education have been taught a lot of misery about heat and cold, so we suffer from the heat and cold and take bad colds, TB, pneumonia, flu, etc.

There are men in Tibet who live in that cold climate way up in the Himalaya Mountains with no heat in their houses. They can sit in the snow on a bitter cold day and enjoy it. One of these men taught his secret to Theos Bernard. They do not feel either heat or cold, good or bad, sickness or health, joy or sorrow, success or failure. They live in the middle road of calm and peace—never up nor down.

Where do diseases come from? Our poisonous badwill thinking brings them into our lives and gives them names. If our badwill thinking had not made them they would not be here at all. Therefore if our thinking caused them, our thinking can stop them.

The flesh and our badwill thoughts about it are all full of misery. There is no lasting harmony in poisonous badwill thoughts about the flesh.

We should always do what we fear we can't do. "Do the thing you fear to do," said Emerson, "and the death of fear is absolutely certain." We can do what we think we can't if we get into a gentle, calm, peaceful mood and let go, let down and let loose of our stubborn belief that we can't do it.

We do not understand the power of a thought. Think of the power of a thought in Thomas Edison that brought into being the electric light, the phonograph, the moving picture! Think of the power of a thought in Alexander Graham Bell that brought us the telephone! Think of the power of a thought in Selton that started the automobile!

Think of the power of a thought in Clara H. Barton which gave us the Red Cross, in Florence Nightingale which gave us nursing, in Mme. Curie which gave us radium!

The power of a thought can change a whole life from sickness to health, from misery to happiness, from fear to fearlessness, from failure to success. Thought is so powerful that we should use it with great care lest we let it ruin our health, our happiness, our success and our life. Remember that soul (will and brain) which does our thinking has in it the gigantic power of God which runs the universe!

Here is the story of a boy who had infantile paralysis. He was taken to a world-famous Vienna surgeon on bone diseases. He gave the boy some simple exercises to do and told him he could get well if he would do them. But did the boy follow the advice? He did not. He would rather drag his leg because it got him the sympathy and coddling of his friends.

We spend no end of time playing golf, swimming. exercising and eating the right food to keep the body healthy. But we never think of doctoring our thought to keep IT healthy. We never think of training our thinking to keep badwill out of it. And yet thinking, free from the 34 badwill poisons, would bring health, happiness, fearlessness and success as nothing else can.

If we try to heal ourselves by driving out the 34 poisons of badwill and fail, think of Thomas Edison. Edison tried 10 thousand times before he found a wire that would stand the heat of the current in his electric light bulb!

Perhaps you think that if we must try 10 thousand times before we get rid of badwill it's too much of a job. But look at the reward! Edison only got an electric light out of his 10 thousand tries but we are going to get health, peace, happiness, daily needs and freedom from fear forever!

Sometimes in doctoring our thought we grow weary and exclaim like Jesus, "My God, why hast Thou forsaken me!" But let us remember that Paul had a thorn in the flesh. He gave thanks for it because it drove him to higher and higher heights of freedom from badwill. It drove him up to higher and higher understanding and joy. Without it Paul might never have grown much above his animal nature. His thorn forced him to be one of the greatest teachers and comforters of mankind, and carried him into heaven.

We won't change from badwill to Goodwill thinking. Then we mourn, "My God, why hast Thou forsaken me?" Sometimes our family won't let disease be healed in us for they don't and won't understand the workings of badwill and Goodwill thinking. Their soggy, fleshly thought dulls the purity of our thinking.

Tuberculosis, cancer, syphilis, heart disease are not as dangerous as badwill. 34 poisons of badwill are the cause of them all. They are only the outer signs of the boiling sewer of badwill that we have turned loose in us. If we could really get rid of 34 poisons of badwill these diseases could not come into our flesh.

Most insane people have healthy bodies because they have no reasoning thought with which to think disease into their bodies. Insane people are usually carefree and happy unless suffering from the gloomy kind of insanity. Therefore their free-hearted thought manufactures healthy, happy bodies and long life. We could do likewise if we were as free from worry, fear and badwill as they are.

When I can't get on top of some sickness, fear, worry, unhappiness or failure I search my thinking to find out what thought is causing my misery. I always find that some thought of mine is doing it, for as I have said, there is always a bad thought that is manufacturing every sickness or trouble.

If, for example, I find that hate, anger, irritation, jealousy, criticism or resentment is causing my trouble, I begin to send out love which melts them all away. If I find pride and selfishness are the cause, I try to become humble and see what I can do to help someone else.

What a blessing it was when I got the gout, for it made me try harder than ever to stop fear and worry which were causing it! I got afraid to fear and worry lest the gout would come back. Sickness, unhappiness and failure are always blessings if we see that they are teaching us to get rid of certain kinds of badwill.

How wonderfully Swedenborg explains that we have a fleshly body with a spiritual body inside of it. Both of these bodies are exactly alike in form and organs, except that one is made out of flesh and the other out of spirit.

Then he shows us that what makes these two bodies tick is our soul (will and thinking). We can will our bodies to be sick and our thinking will obey the order from our will. And our thinking will think our body into sickness.

Or our will can will our bodies to be well and our thinking will obey this order from our will. And our thinking will think our body into health. Our big job is to watch our will and make it will Goodwill thoughts instead of badwill thoughts.

CHAPTER 8

Thankful Thought Heals

IF A MAN gives us a light we say, "Thank you." If a man steps aside to let us pass on the street we say, "Thank you." If a man tells us how to find our way in a strange town we say, "Thank you." And in all these "thank you's" for small favors our heart really feels thankful.

But do we ever give thanks for good health, a good job and the pleasures we have? Do we ever give thanks for a good night's sleep, for the strength to get up in the morning and go to work, for three square meals a day and a place to sleep and clothes to wear? Do we ever give thanks for a good wife and family and home and friends?

Oh no! We thank a man for a light but we never think of giving thanks for the wonderful, everyday things we have. We take them for granted and never see what a "pearl of great price" they are until we lose them. We would willingly give thanks for what we want and haven't got if we could get it. But never a scrap of thanks for what we have. That's merely ours as a matter of course!

Our blessings may not be as many as we would like. Nobody's are. But I learned that I must be deeply thankful for mine such as they are. I found it most helpful to think of someone in worse trouble than I and then give heartfelt thanks that I am as well off as I am. I found great healing in such thankful thought.

What dumb, thankless eggs we are! We have a good job, good health, a good home and more of the good things of life than we rightfully should have. Then if we get a headache or have a poor night's sleep or run into a hot day or get a scolding from the boss we just raise hell! "Ingratitude (thankless-ness), thou marblehearted fiend!"

We who have the most to be thankful for are often not thankful at all. But those who have little to be thankful for, such as a cripple, a blind man or a very poor family, are the really thankful folks. They nearly always have a smile on their faces and we, a frown! A taxi driver and I were watching a man with St. Vitus Dance. As he bobbed up and down along the street, talking and smiling at his friend, the taxi man said, "We don't know when we're well off."

One day I was riding in a taxi to take lunch with our most valuable and likable customer. We were going to have lunch in the finest place to eat in New York. I didn't want to go to the luncheon. No reason for my not wanting to go except pure cussedness.

Not a speck of thanks for being able to ride in the comfort-able, cheerful taxi instead of having to go in the gloomy, noisy, dirty subway! Not a speck of thanks for the blessing of such a big and pleasant customer! No thanks at all for being able to have lunch in the finest restaurant in New York!

As the taxi stopped for a red light at Broadway, a poor, shabby-looking man passed in front of the taxi pushing a wheel chair. In the wheel chair sat another poorly dressed man with no legs. The legless man in the chair was smoking a cigarette with happiness glowing all over his face.

This showed me what a thankless heart I have. Also it warned me that my thankless heart might bring some terrible suffering into my life. And it did. We lost the above most valu-able customer. Every time I get into a sour, thankless mood, it seems to me a cripple or a blind person comes into my view.

A thankless heart is one of the worst kinds of badwill. When we send out this kind of poison it is certain to bring back dis-ease, accidents, unhappiness, fear or failure into our body and our life.

I have given thanks hundreds of times for my sickness, un-happiness, fear and business troubles. That may sound foolish. But pain forces us to go higher in learning and purity than pleasure does. A great trouble in the flesh or in our thought or in business drives us out of the hell of badwill into the heaven of Goodwill thinking.

It drives us out of the ignorance of Self into the understanding of how we can think ourselves into health, happiness, fearlessness and supply of daily needs. That is worth more than a hundred million dollars. Therefore we should give heartfelt thanks for sickness or heartache or fear or business failure.

If we have a terrible disease or trouble it was given to us to wipe out some debt to the law of *Come-Back* and gain some divine gift of heavenly harmony. Therefore we should not mourn about our seeming misfortune. We should give thanks for it. We should see in it the urge and call to heavenly bliss.

People in trouble are liable to say, "How can I give thanks when everything has gone wrong? I have nothing to give thanks for." But there are always many things to be thankful for. We can give thanks that we are still alive, that we are not starving, that we can see and hear, that we are sane, that our hope is not dead, etc., etc.

I was never thankful for anything before I took up the work of doctoring my thought. I saw nothing to be thankful for. My carelessness about giving thanks was a mean, badwill thought. It came back and poisoned me. On the other hand, thankful thoughts would have brought back peace and plenty. The healing power of thankful thought is wonderful.

Shakespeare said, "Ingratitude (thanklessness), sharper than a serpent's tooth." He was talking about ingratitude for favors from our friends. But ingratitude for our blessings also stings us sharper than a serpent's tooth. For ingratitude sends rank poison all through us from head to foot.

We get "sore" and worry about our failure to satisfy our desires. We hate, criticize and grow jealous of those who seem to have more of their desires satisfied than we have. Desire is the cause of most of our badwill thinking. Desire is the cause of thankless thinking. We are thankless because our desires are never satisfied the way we want them to be.

We should take whatever flows to us naturally, whether it be much or little, and be deeply thankful for it. The giving of little or no thanks can bring us nothing but misery.

On the other hand, the giving of thanks is a blessed healer. The healing help we can give ourselves by feeling thankful from way down in our heart is unbelievable until we have tried it. And we should give thanks out loud to others or to ourselves. Giving thanks out loud makes us humble, makes us feel our thankfulness more deeply. So does the giving of thanks on our knees.

The giving of thanks calms us in sickness and opens a big door in our thought through which the power of Goodwill flows in and blesses us. The giving of thanks drowns unhappiness and makes us sweetly satisfied with what we are and what we have. Giving thanks brings balance and wisdom to succeed in business. It melts the clogging dam of thankless thought out of our business path and gives the Holy Spirit of our Lord Jesus a chance to flow our needs to us.

Whenever I feel sour and sunk and the world looks punk I get out a large sheet of paper and draw two columns on it. In one column I write down all my troubles. In the other, all my blessings. The things in the column of blessings are always many and the troubles in the other column few. One look at the two columns makes me sneak back in shame and give thanks for all the good things.

My second teacher told me to hang a sign at the foot of my bed with these words on it I AM THANKFUL so I could see it the first thing when I awoke in the morning. Before I get out of bed in the morning I give thanks for my good sleep and rest. I try to get up singing and giving thanks out loud.

I found it a wonderful healing help to give thanks and sing as much as possible all day. I do this in my all-day prayers. I give thanks for each blessing and not for blessings in general. I name them in detail and I try not to make it lip service. I try to feel heartfelt thanks for each blessing.

When I awake at dawn and hear the orioles, catbirds, song sparrows, wrens, thrushes, robins, tanagers and cardinals all singing a welcome to the new day, it makes me ashamed of myself. For my welcome to the new day has all too often been sour thoughts. Think of it! Sour thoughts for the beautiful, new day so full of chances to do things and help my brothers!

One of the thoughts that used to poison me was jealousy. But when I learned that we are each put here to do a job specially cut out for us, I got over most of my jealousy. I learned that we can't do the other fellow's job and he can't do ours.

Therefore why be jealous of the work of others which we can't do? Or why be jealous of their looks or success which were not given to us by our Lord Jesus (God) who made and runs the universe? The fact is, if somebody is better off than we are that is the business of our Lord Jesus. He knows what is best for us.

Now when I start to be jealous of someone who is having big success in fame or fortune, I say to myself, "Why should you be envious of his success when you know it may bring him poor health and is sure to fill him with fear, worry, sin, unhappiness or boredom?"

If our brother has better health or happiness than we have we should be glad of it. Oh what poison that takes out of us! We can feel the poison flowing out of us.

Let us be thankful for what we have and are. Thankful thought is a powerful healing help. But the rub is to keep thinking thankful thoughts. We may do it for a while. But day by day we will do it less and less until we forget all about it. We should talk and think thankful thoughts before each meal and all day long as often as we can.

In this, as in all branches of doctoring our thought, we have got to watch and work always lest we stray into the hell of poisonous badwill thinking. As I have said, that is what Jesus meant when He spoke the most brief and powerful thought in all history, "Watch."

Thankful thoughts from the bottom of one's heart have the power to pull down mountains of sickness, fear, unhappiness and failure.

CHAPTER 9

Faith

I CAN hear you saying, "This is a wonderful story you are telling. I'd like to believe it but I don't. How can I get faith in it?" We will never get faith in the power of Goodwill thinking until we try it and see it work. It WILL work if we try it with all our heart.

But most of us try Goodwill thinking with only a little of our heart in it. We try it dishonestly. We don't want to give up any of our 34 badwill poisons. Then when the power of Goodwill can't work through our badwill thinking and give us health, happiness and plenty we say, "How can I have faith?"

Experience with the workings of Goodwill thinking more than anything else will make us believe in it. For as we see Goodwill thinking change our health and life for the better, our faith will grow stronger and stronger and our belief in the power of the flesh to harm us will get weaker and weaker. Thus we will slowly become willing to put our trust in the power of Goodwill thinking.

Edison got faith in the unseen power of electricity by proving again and again that it would work. Just so we get faith in what the unseen power of Goodwill thinking does for us.

Faith in the power of Goodwill thinking "is more to be desired than gold, yea, than much fine gold" or diamonds or any riches that the world has to give. For understanding of the workings of Goodwill thinking and faith in it bring health, peace, happiness and daily needs now and forever. More wealth than these no one can desire.

This greatest wealth in all the universe cannot be gained by merely wanting it. We've got to be willing to work for it.

To give in and be willing to have faith is the hard thing for us to do. We are not willing even though we think we are.

If we can't get faith in the boundless power that runs the universe and ourselves, then there is nothing left for us to do but put our trust in badwill. We know in our hearts that we can't trust badwill. We know that if we depend on it we must live a life of illness, fear, misery and failure.

Those who are willing to believe in the power of Goodwill thinking can be helped or healed and made happy and supplied with what they need. But those who are not willing must suffer until they ARE willing.

Four soldiers were in a dugout during World War I. One of them believed that if he had faith in the power of Goodwill thinking the Germans wouldn't see him because they couldn't see good with their fleshly eyes full of badwill. He got away unharmed but the other three were shot. His faith took care of him.

How miserable and hopeless we feel in our hearts when we try to have no faith. That alone should prove that we are all wrong when we try to have no faith. My heart bleeds whenever I meet a man who stiffens up proudly and tries to prove that there is nothing in the power of Goodwill thinking.

He says he is too "hard boiled" to believe such mushy stuff. If he could only know the difference between his miserable, dull life of badwill thinking and the joy and peace and melody that come from the gentle, loving power of Goodwill thoughts! "He that doubteth is like the waves of the sea, driven by the wind and tossed."

We who think we are too "hard boiled" to believe really are as hard as granite in our hearts and our thinking. We receive nothing but badwill thoughts from hell.

Toyohiko Kagowa is a tiny, sickly Japanese champion of religion. He has caused a great change in the religious thinking of the Japanese people. Mr. Kagowa has suffered sickness, pain and the bitterest of sorrow in his work to help his people.

Yet he says that through all his heart-breaking experiences he felt a loving peace inside of him that nothing could stamp out. Even when his eyes were shot out in a riot against his loving work for the poor in the slums, he said this peace within could not be upset. He said it stayed there inside of him unmoved like a heavenly light, ever glowing comfort, support and cheer.

We all know that some power inside of us heartens us and keeps us up through our hardest trials. What is it? It is the Holy Spirit in our heart from Our Lord. It always comes and helps us. Most of us have felt it as Kagowa did.

Where does the beauty of flowers and trees and all nature come from? From the everlasting harmony of Our Lord Jesus (God) who created and runs the universe. Seeming enemies and seasons try to strike them down but they always come back and beautify the earth and glow their love to us. That alone should give us faith in this loving power that never fails.

We know there is a great power, for we feel it in our heart. We can't get it out of our heart. Our heart longs for a great power to mother us. Our heart won't let us believe there is no such power. Unbelievers may try as they will to stamp out the belief in our Lord Jesus (God). But this longing for a power to mother us will "spring eternally in the human breast."

As a child we lean on our father and mother who gave us a fleshly body. All our lives we feel the need of a father and mother or power greater than ourselves to lean on. Why do we feel this longing? Because we know in our hearts that there IS a universal Father and we have strayed away from Him into a strange and dangerous land of wrong thinking.

Look at the faces and bodies of the 2 billion human beings on the earth! No two of them alike, not even twins. Even the style of walking of each of these 2 billions of people is so different that we know a man afar off by his style of walking even when we can't see his face.

Look at the birds which have no power to think! They travel thousands of miles north and south twice a year to the same nest. What guides these little feathered beings to do such miracles?

Look at the grandeur of the sunset or the moon rising out of the sea! Look at the perfection of a flower, a tree or a bird and the endless variety of them! "Consider the lilies; they toil not, neither do they spin, and yet Solomon in all his glory was not arrayed like one of these."

Lie down flat on the ground and look up at the sky and ask yourself who made all that boundless ceiling of blue. When we look at Niagara Falls, or the azaleas at Charleston, or the Grand Canyon of the Colorado, what does their grandeur say to us? It says that only a kind of thinking vastly greater than our little thoughts could have made them.

When our faith weakens we should look at the stars and say, "What right have we with our peewee thinking to doubt that there is a gigantic Mind which built this gigantic universe and runs it?" The vast thinking of our Lord Jesus (God) is far beyond our understanding. Therefore it is really silly for us to doubt that there is such a God. Our doubt only proves how shallow our own proud little thinking is.

Read these lines from Otto J. Klink's booklet WHY I AM NOT AN ATHEIST (one who doesn't believe there is a God):

"This globe of ours is so small that it would take 1,200,-000 earths to make the sun. If you could throw our little planet into the sun it would be like throwing a match into a burning furnace.

"And we know that the Polar Star is 1 thousand times bigger than our sun. Sirus, the largest of the fixed stars, is 5 thousand times bigger than the sun. Boga is 54 thousand times bigger than the sun and Arcturus is 550 thousand times larger than the sun. Who made all that? Chance, says the atheist.

"*** With the naked eye you can see about 5 thousand stars; with an opera-glass you can see 13 thousand; with a small telescope about 100 thousand; with a large telescope 1 million; with a still larger one 45 million; and if you look as I did, through the great refracting telescope at Treptow, that is 21 meters long, you can see 100 million stars.***

"As far as human reckoning goes there circle overhead about 1,200 million suns. And how immensely far away from us are these worlds. An express train that would reach the moon in 7 months would have to speed along 233 years without stopping to arrive at the sun.

"I look out yonder at old Mars, 260 million miles away,

traveling around the sun once in 687 days, or in about 2 years, going at the speed of 49 thousand miles an hour. Jupiter is 480 million miles away; Saturn, 885 million miles away. He travels around the sun once in 20 years, going at the speed of 21 thousand miles an hour.

"Then there is old Uranus, 1 billion 7 hundred 80 thousand miles away. Too far for the naked eye to see is old Neptune. It would take you 3 thousand years to get there in an aeroplane flying 100 miles an hour. She goes around the sun once in 165 years. She is 3 billion miles away.*** The North Star is 400 billion miles away from the earth. A fast plane could fly there in about 400 million years.

"Who conceived all this? Who brought all this into existence? Who runs all this colossal universe in silent harmony with planets speeding at 49 thousand miles an hour and none of them ever in collision or in anything but quiet, blissful rhythm?

"Atheists tell us that these laws that keep the rolling worlds in their orbits (paths) so that they move on without jar and jostle have been formulated without a law-giver; in some unthinkable, haphazard way they have made themselves!

"I am not an atheist," says Mr. Klink, "because I believe where there is a creation there must be a Creator."

Mr. Klink failed to tell of the startling fact that the earth speeds around the sun at the rate of 18.6 miles a second or 66,960 miles an hour. We with our little shallow thinking look with wonder on a plane which can make 600 miles an hour!

We have little or no experience in things divine yet we set ourselves up as judges and proudly air our silly doubts.

We don't have faith because we do not understand what our self is. We do not understand what our "I" is. We think our "I" is the flesh. We think our body is the "I." But our "I" is none of these things.

Our "I" is our Soul (will and thinking). And our soul is from our Lord Jesus (God). Our lack of faith is due to the fact that we are trying to have faith in body and flesh which are false, fleeting things to have faith in.

There are 3 grades of thinking; namely, the lowest or fleshly grade of thinking. Then the grade where we try to see through everything by arguments or reasoning. Then the third and highest grade far above all arguments and reasoning where we know all things and feel the truth about ourself without having to think it out.

This highest grade of thinking has come over me now and then. When it did so, I knew that there is a beautiful, unseen power. I knew it without reasoning it out. For example: At times when I have been able to overcome a lot of my badwill, a tenderness, sweetness and love seem to come in and spread all through me like soft moonlight. Whenever I feel this bliss I am filled with a deep faith that is far beyond all doubts and arguments. Millions of people have had this baptism of tenderness and love. It is the Holy Spirit from our Lord Jesus (God) working in us.

I recall an experience of this kind which I shall never forget. It was only a few weeks after I had taken up Christian Science. I was on a train up New York State in a lightning storm.

At that time I was full of fear—afraid of being away from home—afraid of the train I was on and scared stiff of the lightning. My panic got so bad I didn't think I could hold myself down. I was afraid I would jump off the train.

As I thought I was about to go to pieces with nervousness I decided to sit down and try to pray. I had never done this before and therefore didn't know how to go about it. I sat down in the parlor car, closed my eyes and was saying to myself silently, "There is only one God," etc.

Suddenly it seemed to me I saw the face of Jesus and He seemed to be saying to me silently, "Peace, be still. Lo, I am with you always, even unto the end of the world." Quick as a flash all my fear left me. I was as calm as the sea after a storm and a heavenly peace was flowing all through me.

That night and for weeks afterward I was entirely free from all fear. This miracle filled me with a childlike faith which has never left me. Another experience that overwhelmed me with faith is a book entitled "George Mueller of Bristol." Mueller raised $7,500,000 for his orphan homes by prayer alone. Never asked any man for one penny. Mueller could trust the Lord. A friend of mine born in Bristol, Eng., says this story is all true.

Here is a story I read in a magazine. It always fills me with faith that we CAN break through the veil of badwill and feel the love and presence of the Holy Spirit of Our Lord Jesus.

The story is about a soldier who lay dying in the Moroccan desert. The fight, a mere skirmish, was over, the enemy beaten off and the members of his troop had not found him in the place where he had fallen. The hot desert sand was under him; the heartless desert sun beat on him where he lay. His wounds made every breath an agony but a greater suffering still was his thirst. And he was alone!

But he really wasn't alone. Through the fever and the pain and the mercifully-increasing weakness he felt a presence beside him. First it was like a shadow that shaded him from the sun; then as a cool breath of air; and the coolness lay upon his mouth like water from a mountain stream and he had a dream of snow-clad heights and he heard the sound of the mountain torrent which seemed to wash over him and bathe his wounds.

Then the sound of the water became the sound of a voice— O that voice! He could not hear what it said—he was far too weak for that; but it was healing and comforting—it was the love of all his loved ones mingled together but above and beyond anything he had ever known before. After that, strong arms pillowed his head and the voice came closer and closer until he fell asleep in wonder and perfect peace.

He woke up presently in heaven. But he was not satisfied. "Give me," he said, "the desert sands and the burning sun and the wounds and the thirst that I may have again that presence beside me and hear that voice—that voice is what I want but what it was saying to me I do not know." And so, the story goes, the soldier broke through, out of his heaven, so great was his desire for that which he had lost, and he found the master who had nursed him.

The Master was one of his two guardian angels. For two angels follow each one of us day and night to help us and guard us from evil spirits. Or it might have been the Lord Jesus Himself.

If we sincerely try to stop all badwill our guardian angels

will come to each one of us, and help us, guide us and comfort us on our hard climb to heaven. Almost daily I am utterly amazed to see problems of all kinds melt into harmony without my doing anything about them save to wait until an urge moves me to act. Often I cannot see the wisdom of what I do until after I do it. These astonishing experiences give me unbounded faith.

I give below an experience of a woman who had never made any study of Christian Science or of training her thought. This experience is so beautiful that it will bring faith to any heart that is humbly willing to have faith.

Margaret Prescott Montague, authoress, had the experience and told about it in the *Atlantic Monthly*. She called it "Twenty Minutes of Reality."

She said that it happened to her on a day when her bed was first pushed out of doors onto the open porch of a hospital. She was getting over an operation. She had suffered from physical pain and says for a short time she had fallen into the deepest gloom in her whole life.

She said that while she was under the ether and out of her head in the operating room she seemed to have found a terrible secret—that there was no God, or, if there was one, He did not care if people suffered. The blackness of that gloom had faded and only a little fear was left when several days later her bed was wheeled out onto the sunporch.

It was an ordinary, cloudy March day, almost a dingy day. The tree branches were bare and colorless and the half-melted piles of snow were a friendless gray. Colorless little city sparrows flew and chirped in the trees. Here it was, she said, in this everyday scene that entirely by surprise she caught sight of the joyous beauty of reality—the beyond.

She could not say exactly what the queer change was or whether it came quickly or slowly. She saw no new thing but saw all the usual things in a strange new light—in what she believed was their true light. She saw for the first time how madly beautiful and joyous beyond any words of hers to tell it is the whole of life.

It was not for a few keyed-up moments that she fancied all

existence to be beautiful but her inner sight was cleared to the truth so that she saw the real loveliness which is always there but which we so rarely see; and she saw that every man, woman, bird and tree, every living thing before her was divinely beautiful and divinely important.

A nurse was walking past; the wind caught a strand of her hair and blew it out into a gleam of sunshine and never in her life before had she seen how beautiful beyond all belief was a woman's hair. A little sparrow chirped and flew to a nearby branch and she said she honestly believed that "only the morning stars singing together and the sons of God shouting for joy" could in the least way picture the joyous beauty of a bird's flight. She could not tell it in words but she saw it.

Only this once out of all the gray days of her life had she looked into the heart of the beyond; she had witnessed the truth; she had seen life as it really is—delightfully, joyfully, madly beautiful and filled to overflowing with a wild, unbelievable gladness.

She was aware, too, of a wonderful feeling of soft, swinging movement, only somehow it was just beyond the grasp of her thought. She heard no music, yet there was a beautiful sense of time as though all life went by to a vast, unseen melody. Everything that moved wove out a little thread of soft-swinging movement in this great Whole.

When a bird flew it did so because somewhere a note had been struck for it to fly on; or else its flying struck the note; or else again the great Will that is melody willed that it should fly.

Then the vast importance of everything! It seemed as though before her very eyes she actually beheld the truth of Christ's saying that not even a sparrow falls to the ground without the knowledge of the Father in heaven. Yet what the importance was she did not grasp. If her heart could have seen just a little further she might have understood.

Even now the tips of her thoughts are forever on the verge of grasping it, forever just missing it. It was perhaps as though the great value in every living thing was not so much here and now in ourselves as somewhere else. There is a great meaning in every little thing in the universe but the meaning is beyond our present grasp.

What if here we are only echoes of ourselves and our real being is somewhere else—perhaps in the heart of God? Certainly that unbelievable importance had to do with our kinship to the Whole. But she could not tell what the kinship was. Was it a kinship of love toward us?

For those fleeting, lovely moments she said she did indeed love her neighbor as herself. Nay more—she was madly in love with everything from wind-tossed branches and little sparrows flying, up to human beings. She wondered if it was likely that she could have experienced such love if there were not some such thing as love at the heart of reality.

Her experience, she thought, was a sort of unexpected clearing of her sight at the rebirth of returning health.

She said that doubtless almost any deep feeling may open our "inward eye" to the beauty of reality. Falling in love appears to do it for some people. The beauties of nature or the thrill of bringing something artistic into being does it for others. She says that poets are not dreaming the joyous beauty of which they sing. They are telling us the truth that is there when they are now and then able to see it.

Probably any high experience may for a moment stretch our souls so that we catch a glimpse of that marvelous beauty which is always there but which we are not often tall enough to see. Emerson says that we are sunk in beauty but our eyes have no clear sight to see it.

In what she saw there seemed to be nothing of a moral nature. There were no rules for being good. Indeed, she said that it seemed as though beauty and joy were more at the heart of reality than morality. Perhaps at such times when heaven is unveiled there is no need to worry over sin, for one is so changed by the beauty of humanity and so full of love toward every human being that sin becomes almost impossible. She hopes that perhaps some day again the gray veil of unreality will be swirled and once more she may see into reality. One day in her garden the veil was very thin. The wind was blowing there and she knew that all the wild, young joy at the

heart of life was rioting with it through the tossing larkspurs
and rose-pink Canterbury bells and bowing with the foxgloves
—only she just could not see it.

But she said it is always there—it is always there forever
singing to us and we are forever failing to dance. We could
not help but dance if we could see things as they really are.
Then we would kiss both hands to fate and throw our bodies,
hearts, thoughts and souls into life with a glorious freedom
from care, a joyous, delighted faith. We would know that our
wildest dreams of fairyland cannot more than brush the hem
of the real beauty and joy and wonder that are always there.

This is how, for her, all fear of the hereafter was wiped away.
She said that even if there were no other life, this life here
and now, if we could but open our dull eyes to see it, is lovely
enough to need no far-off heaven to satisfy us. That heaven is
here now, before our very eyes, rolling up to our very feet,
beating against our very hearts—but we, alas, know not how
to let it in!

Sadhu Sundar Singh saw all this when his spiritual vision was
opened about eight times a month. Swedenborg saw it thousands of times when his spiritual body traveled in the heavens
and talked with angels.

Faith is complete trust in our Lord Jesus (God) for everything. For our life here, our health, our food, our income, our
life after death. It means leaning on Him alone to do everything
for us with NO RELIANCE ON OURSELF as George
Mueller did. Merely believing that there is a God is not FAITH.
It is shallow belief and in most cases the belief is of the lips and
not of the heart.

CHAPTER 10

Death

MAYBE you don't believe the Old Testament where it tells how the prophets and people talked with Jehovah—God. Maybe you don't believe the New Testament which tells how Peter, James, John and Jesus went up into the Mount and talked with Moses and Elijah.

If you don't, let's consider modern people who see into our next life and who walk and talk with folks over there. Some of these humans are still here with us. Some of them I know.

For example: I know Edith Ellis who lives in New York. She is an honest, sincere woman with no purpose in life except to help others. I have talked to her in her home many times.

She talks to Wilfred Brandon in our next life. She writes down what he tells her. He dictated three books to her; namely, OPEN THE DOOR, INCARNATION and WE KNEW THESE MEN.

In these books Brandon tells how he lives in our next life and many other interesting things. He tells how those who die are received into our next life and taught how to live in their new life by the White Brotherhood over there, of which he is a member.

Edith Ellis has also taken long messages from George Washington, Lincoln, Jefferson, Theodore Roosevelt and many other famous statesmen who are living in our next life.

Also I know Howell S. Vincent. He is now living in Homossassa Springs, Fla. He was a missionary in China for 25 years. Mr. Vincent would never write an untruth. Three days after his daughter was married, she and her husband were fatally hurt in an automobile accident.

Dr. Vincent and his family watched their children pass into glory in our next life. They even saw their daughter fall into the arms of her mother (Vincent's first wife who had passed on before).

They saw the spiritual funeral (resurrection) hovering over the fleshly funeral of the children. The spiritual funeral (resurrection) was joyous with music, angels and beautiful singing brides. They talked to their children many times after their death. Mr. Vincent tells all about it in his book LIGHTED PASSAGE.

Mrs. Alfred Payson Terhune, wife of the famous writer of dog stories who died only a short time ago, talked with her departed husband many times. She tells all about her talks with him in her book ACROSS THE LINE.

Then there is a book called VOICES FROM THE OPEN DOOR by Mrs. T. F. Hauts of San Francisco. She died only a few years ago. Her niece, Mrs. Watson, lives near us. Often comes to see us. Her niece and others who knew Mrs. Hauts say she was a beautiful Christian. In VOICES FROM THE OPEN DOOR she tells in detail of 31 talks she had with people in our next life.

Then there is the case of Sadhu Sundar Singh. He is a Hindu but probably the purest Christian alive (if he is still alive). He hasn't been heard from since he went into Tibet some years ago. He wrote a book called VISIONS OF THE SPIRITUAL WORLD. In it he says these words:

". . . At Kotgarh (India) fourteen years ago while I was praying, my eyes were opened to the heavenly vision. So vividly did I see it all that I thought I must have died and that my soul had passed into the glory of heaven.

". . . But throughout the intervening years, these visions have continued to enrich my life. I cannot call them up at will. But usually when I am praying or meditating, sometimes as often as 8 or 10 times a month, my spiritual eyes are opened to see within the heavens.

". . . The answers of angels to my questions x x x x and

the unutterable ecstacy of that spiritual communion makes me long for the time when I shall enter in permanently to the bliss and fellowship of the redeemed."

Then I studied the findings of spiritualism. I found that spiritual mediums have proved both in England and America that they can talk with those who have "died." They can even bring their bodies into a seance (meeting of spiritualists). They can do it because the mediums have perfect pituitary and pineal glands. I found they have been proving life after "death" for 50 years. They have thousands of books and pamphlets telling of talks, messages and visions from our next life.

Maybe you don't believe what is seen and heard at spiritual seances. Well, here are some mighty able minds who did believe it: Sir Oliver Lodge, Professor Crooks (a leading English scientist), William Stead (eminent English editor), Maurice Maeterlinck (distinguished author), Lord Balfour, William James, Sir Conan Doyle, etc., etc.

However, dear friends, may we advise you not to attend spiritual seances? We dislike saying anything against them for they have done the world a splendid service in proving that we live after "death." And there are noble hearts who practice as spiritual mediums.

If you care to know more about the danger of being a spiritual medium or going to seances, read THE GREAT PSYCHOLOGICAL CRIME by T. K. Also we would advise you not to read a lot of books about our next life. For many of these books, even in libraries, contain things which may not be true. These "fables" may upset you.

But no harm can come to us from reading the above mentioned books.

Only good can come from gaining enlightenment from good books. For "The whole purpose of life is enlightenment."

But the peak of all my studies about life after death came when I began to read the books of Emanuel Swedenborg. For the three heavens were opened to him. He saw everything in them. He talked with angels thousands of times. He says that the spiritual meaning of the word death is not death but resurrection.

Our fleshly body houses our spiritual body which is inside of our fleshly body. It houses our spiritual body until the fleshly body wears out. When our fleshly body has lost its usefulness our spiritual body throws it off like we discard an old overcoat. Then our deathless, eternal, spiritual body goes into our next life and lives on forever. This I am sure is the Truth about death.

CHAPTER 11

Fear

I WAS always afraid of something even in my childhood. Afraid of thunderstorms, afraid of dogs, afraid to ride behind horses, afraid of railroad accidents, afraid of snakes, afraid of seeing injured people or dead people, afraid I would go insane, afraid of about everything.

These fears were all caused by dreadful things that happened to me in my childhood and by the fears of my parents.

For example: My mother was afraid of thunderstorms; my brother and I were bitten by dogs; a runaway of a horse and buggy nearly killed a woman in front of our house; railroad accidents in my childhood days were as common as aeroplane accidents today; a snake wound around a playmate's leg; a dead man, killed in a railroad accident, was brought in right before my eyes; and I feared insanity because of the sex habit of youth.

Doctors of thought, called psychiatrists, dig up all the causes of childhood fears now-a-days. Then they show a grown-up person how silly it is to let these foolish fears of childhood haunt him in manhood. By this method many people are greatly helped.

Parents should use painstaking care to raise children free from fear. If I were raising children again I would send them to a Christian Science Sunday School or to a Unity or New Thought Sunday School or to the Sunday School of the Church of the Healing Christ. For they fill the child's simple thought with the understanding that there is nothing to fear.

To enjoy a fearless childhood is one of the most precious gifts that parents can give to a child. Because the fears we take into the tender thinking of childhood are liable to stick to us and scare us all our lives.

After my breakdown at the age of 32 I worked up an alarming fear and nervousness about myself. The first thing it did was to make me afraid of closed places, like elevators, subways or any place where I was not free to get out if I wanted to.

Then I got afraid to ride on express trains because they ran for a long time without stopping. This bottled me up for hours in a car where I could not get out if I wished to. Also I worked up a fear of sleeping away from home at night. In both cases I was afraid I might go wild and not be able to hold myself down.

I feared that this might cause a scene in a train or hotel. The heartache of this fear of trains and sleeping in hotels away from home was cruel for I had to travel or close up my business. I could not give up the business because I had a family to raise. So I had to suffer from these fears for 19 years.

But when I got back home the fears went away and I was free. However, fear that is not broken up grows worse, so I began to take on more fears. I began to be afraid at home, as well as away from home. I got so nervous at night that I feared I could not hold myself in bed. I was afraid I would lose control of myself and hurt somebody.

The evenings which I had always enjoyed so much at home grew unbearable. I could not relax after dinner and enter into the happy circle of my family. I felt so tight and keyed up that I couldn't let loose and sit comfortably even in a soft arm chair.

I had tried for 19 years in Christian Science to break these fears by denying them and fighting them and declaring that they were not real. Then after supposedly knocking the devils out of me I tried to believe that "perfect love casteth out fear." This way of doctoring my thought failed to get rid of my fears. It only brushed them aside for a little while but, like the cat, they always came back.

This is no criticism of Christian Science or of my beloved Christian Science teacher. I alone was at fault. As I was about to go to pieces I went to another teacher (a doctor of thought). She taught me the following way to help nervousness and fear:

She told me to tell her out loud what I was afraid of. I did. I said, "I am afraid of everything." She said, "That is no admission of fear. That's merely a covering up of fear." She said, "I want you to tell me each thing you are afraid of and tell it to me right out loud." Of course I wouldn't do it. I tried to. I wanted to. But something inside of me wouldn't let me.

I asked her, "Why am I unwilling to tell someone else what I am afraid of out loud?" "Because," she said, "fear is a secret thing. It wants to work secretly and silently inside of us. It doesn't want to be brought out into the light where its folly would look so foolish that we would laugh at it and let go of it."

I learned that we are really ashamed of our fears. We are ashamed of being so yellow. So we stubbornly refuse to tell anybody what our fears are. Therefore we just let them boil inside of us and eat the heart out of us rather than admit them out loud.

I said to myself, "Why should I tell someone else what I am afraid of out loud?" Here is the answer: The science of psychiatry (study of the workings of thought) has proved that if a sufferer from fear will admit what he is afraid of out loud to himself, or better still to someone else, he will lose nearly all his fear.

I finally did grow willing enough to tell someone else out loud that I was afraid of closed places, kidnaping, business failure, insanity, being away from home and death. I can't tell you what a load that lifted off of me. The moment I told all these fears out loud to another person they seemed to suddenly go away.

If you doubt this method of modern psychiatry try it on yourself. It is not mere fancy. It is a proven method used by psychiatrists and in hospitals where they doctor diseases of the nerves and diseases that upset our power to think.

I heard of a woman who was afraid she would scream in a public place and create a scene. This woman was advised to go out into the country where nobody could hear her and scream until she got it all out. She did so and never again suffered from the fear of screaming. Fear pent up inside of us is like steam in a boiler which has no safety valve to let it blow off. If we don't give the fear a chance to get out it will grow in size until it blows us up. Fear scares us because we don't let it out.

It is better to confess what we are afraid of to someone else than to ourself. But if no one is present, as in the dead of night, we can make the confession to ourself but we should always do it out loud.

When I got a spell of fear at night I was advised to get out of bed, turn on the light, point my finger at myself in a mirror and say out loud, "What the hell are you afraid of?" Then confess to myself out loud each thing that I was afraid of.

I was told to go back to bed then and not fight the fear or the nervousness or whatever was scaring me. Instead, I was advised to say to myself, "I am willing to lie down here on this nice bed in this nice room. I am willing to be thankful."

I was told to lie there quietly and give thanks for everything I could think of and to name each thing for which I was thankful and do it all quietly, slowly and silently.

I tried this advice. I could not make it work at first because I was not really willing to, although I thought I was. But little by little I began to be willing. Then I was surprised to find that I would relax, let go, let down, let loose and fall asleep. My night fear grew less and less until finally one day I thought to myself, "Why, this night fear has all gone away!"

I remember one night I was trying to sleep on an island far out to sea. There was only one boat a day to the mainland. Before I went there I feared being out there so far away from everything.

In the middle of the night I was overcome with the fear I had built up about being so far away from the mainland. I tried to heal the fear with all the ways of doctoring my thought that I knew. But none of them gave me relief. I grew panicky.

Then I recalled what I was told to do when all the doctoring of my thought had failed to wipe out my fear. I remembered that I had been taught to sit down and write something like the following 100 times on a pad of paper:

"I don't have to be this way. I can change. I am willing to change. I am willing to let go of this selfish thinking of myself. I am willing to stop thinking ONLY of my own comfort. I am willing to go insane or even die if necessary to break up this fear."

I sat up in bed and wrote these lines 100 times. At the end of the 100 writings all the nervousness and fear left me and a blessed peace stole all through me. I fell into a deep sleep until 8 o'clock the next morning when I awoke fully rested and refreshed.

This way of writing sickness, fear and worry out of one's thought is a marvelous way to relieve these sufferings. It gives us something to lean on when we are scared and all other ways of doctoring our thought have failed.

It breaks up the whirling of our thought on the fear that is scaring us. And when that whirling gets broken up the fear goes away. It takes a lot of willingness to do this hard job of writing but the peace it brings is sweet.

Sometimes we can quiet our fear by reading and thus save ourselves the hard work of all this writing. Try reading first. If that fails, do the writing. But we should not read anything that stirs us up like fiction. That will get us wider awake. Read some dry, heavy book.

If we ever wish to use this way of writing fear out of our thought it is not necessary to follow the above wording exactly. Word the lines to fit whatever kind of badwill you are trying to overcome.

We should remember that everything is changing all the time. Our bodies are changing, stones and plants are changing. Even the stars and the universe are changing every moment. Just so our thoughts are always changing. Therefore our fear thoughts will change if we stop hanging on to them like a bulldog. The above way of doctoring our thought helps to break up the hanging on and then our thought changes and the fear goes away.

I once got the gout. The pain in my big toe joint was so terrible one night that I could hardly bear it. The dope the doctor gave me failed to stop it. So I got out my pad of paper and doctored my thought by writing. Before I had finished the 100 writings I was relieved and fell asleep.

I learned how to let go and "unlax" after dinner at night. I found that I had been keying myself up with such high-strung feelings of strife and strain, irritation and anger all day long that when I got home at night I could not let loose and relax.

Then I got afraid of my tight, rigid feelings. This fear and the tight feelings kept me in a strain all evening. So I began to carry on my business during the day in a more quiet way. These more quiet days carried quiet, loose feelings into my evenings and brought back peace and pleasure after dinner at night. If one is inclined to be high-strung he should not smoke or drink liquor, coffee, tea or cola drinks, for they string us up and make it harder to let down.

I learned how to ease or overcome the fear of closed places and the fear of riding on trains and sleeping away from home. I found that this panicky fear was caused by irritation, anger and the high-strung way I worked. I kept myself in such a high pitch of strain that when I had to remain quiet in a closed place I couldn't let myself down and let loose. This made me panicky.

Another reason for my fear of these closed places was this: I was used to ruling everything with my badwill. When I found myself in a closed place which I couldn't rule, that made me afraid of it. Then I resisted it and fought it with badwill. This fighting fought back at me and the comeback of the fighting scared me and made me afraid of the closed place.

Now when I get panicky in these closed places I get quiet and sweet inside and try to let loose all over. I close my eyes and say to myself, "I am willing to be here. I am willing to be thankful for this useful elevator or subway or train or hotel room. I am willing to neither fight nor resist them. I am willing to let go, let loose and enjoy them. I am willing to believe that my thought can change and be thankful for them." Then I keep repeating the 91st Psalm and remember that by repeating and believing it a whole British regiment never lost a man in 4 years.

Little by little this feeling of quietness inside of me and trust in the 91st Psalm began to make the fear of closed places melt away. I can see now that when I used to get these panicky feelings I didn't know how to handle them.

I had simply been stirring up the fear more and more by denying it and by repeating "Perfect love casteth out fear" like a parrot. This sort of doctoring of my thought only made my old badwill more tight, strained and fearful until I felt that I would blow up and become dangerous unless I could get out of the closed place.

But when I would let loose, relax and trust in the protection of the 91st Psalm, my fighting against the closed place would weaken and my frightened thought would quiet down and let go. Then the panicky feeling in the closed place would ease up or go away.

When we get scared in a closed place or away from home, our great need is to sidetrack OUR WILL and let the loving WILL of our Lord Jesus (God) work. Our will is straining and storming or we would not be scared of the closed place. The *Will* of our Lord Jesus is always calm and peaceful. Get His quiet will to working instead of OUR boiling, raging will and the panic over the closed place will change to a soft feeling of "peace, be still." We should keep saying to ourselves silently in the closed place, "Be still and know that I am God."

Our Lord Jesus (God) will never let us suffer more than we can bear. That's why He appeared to me in my panic on the train near Canajoharie, N. Y. That's why He appeared to Starr Daly in the dungeon. That's why He appeared to Sadu Sundar Singh when he was about to commit suicide.

One of the greatest doctors who ever lived told me that people who fear closed places or fear being alone or away from home have no disease of the brain. The fear, he said, is merely a nervous notion that amounts to nothing. He told me at the time I had so much fear of trains to get on a train that didn't stop between New York and San Francisco. I said, "Won't anything happen to me?" He replied, "Not a thing."

My first teacher said, "The panic that flashes over you in a closed place or when you are away from home goes away quickly and therefore you should not get scared of it." I found this was absolutely true. The flashes of fear came and went and finally stopped. So what difference does it make if we have a few flashes of fear? Let them come and go and die out!

Many people who are full of fear or "nerves" get the notion that they will never get over it. I held fast to the thought that I COULD get well and I did. We should never hold the thought that we can't get well from any disease.

But the most important thing that helped me to quiet these fears was my awakening to the fact that I really enjoyed them. I thought I wanted to get rid of them but I really didn't. I actually got pleasure out of stewing about fear and nervousness and out of the sympathy I got from my family. It had become a habit—a little racket of mine.

When I got tired of my little racket and suffered enough I decided to let go of the habit of fear and then I got relief. Without knowing it we hold on to sickness, misery, fear and failure. We don't know that we don't want to get rid of them. But when we decide to dump them we will. We won't believe this until we have gone through it.

Hardly any of our fears ever come true. Fear is nearly always about nothing. We are not afraid of something; we are nearly always afraid of nothing. When something really worthy of fear comes up we meet it and drive it away. We don't fear it.

Lightning struck two houses I lived in on the seashore during two different summers. These shattering experiences, plus my childhood fear of thunderstorms, sank me deep into the fear of lightning.

I made a study of the danger of thunderstorms and found them to be about the least dangerous thing in life. There is only about one chance in a billion that lightning will ever strike our house. Even if it should, there is only about one chance in a million that it will harm anyone in the house.

There is no danger at all if we are in a steel-built apartment house or office building, for the lightning goes into the ground through the steel frame of the building. The Empire State

Building and other skyscrapers are often struck but nobody in the building knows of it.

Lightning rods, if built according to the rules of the Government Bureau of Standards, carry the bolts of lightning into the ground and thus may keep them from harming us or our house. It is claimed that no house protected with rods put on in accordance with the rules of the Bureau of Standards has ever been damaged by lightning.

There is no danger from thunder. Thunder is merely a loud noise caused by air rushing in to fill up the hole burnt into the air by the streak of lightning.

Perhaps no fear ever gnawed at my heart worse than the fear of insanity. This dread was caused by my parents who warned me that the sex habit of youth would bring insanity upon me. It was also caused by reading a booklet on the subject in my teens.

I was too shy to ask a doctor about the habit or to admit it to my parents. I prayed and suffered secret sorrow and agony for many years. Finally my parents saw my trouble and sent me to a kind old doctor who relieved my fear and helped me to overcome wet dreams.

How my heart bleeds for the youth who suffers from this horror and for parents who know not how to handle it! If a girl or boy does not overdo this habit it will do no harm. The boy or girl and parents should learn that this habit comes from evil spirits in the hells of our next life. These spirits had strong appetites for sex when they were in their fleshly bodies on earth.

In their spiritual bodies in our next life they cannot have sex. Therefore they seek sex delight by tempting us on earth to revel in sex. They can see us but we can't see them. They get a kind of sex satisfaction by seeing us in the act of sex here.

The only way to stop this sex habit is for parents to pray as follows: "Our Father Lord Jesus which art in heaven. If it be Thy will please have mercy on John Doe (or Mary Doe) at 10 Smith Street, Dover, N. J. And please have mercy on all their brothers and sisters who, like them, are suffering from the sex habit of youth.

"Dear Lord Jesus, if it be Thy will, please have Thy perfect

life command the evil spirits to come out of John Doe of 10
Smith Street, Dover, N. J., and out of all his brothers and sisters who are suffering from the sex habit of youth.

"And dear Lord Jesus, if it be Thy will, please command the
evil spirits to come out of them and enter no more into them
forever. I thank thee Lord Jesus that Thou has heard me for I
know that this is being done." John Doe should pray also, if
he will.

Have faith in this prayer and the evil spirits will come out of
John Doe and "go into the herd of swine: and the whole herd
of swine will run violently down a steep place into the sea and
perish in the waters." (Sea means hell.) They will flee from
John Doe as they did when Jesus commanded the evil spirits
to come out of the man "possessed with devils." But unless we
believe in this prayer it will not free John Doe.

I have been amazed how this prayer works. It works against
enemies also. And may relieve disease. If you don't get an answer to this prayer at once, keep on praying. Don't ever give
up and stop praying.

Above all don't be bashful about sex or the habit of youth.
Tell your parents or your doctor or a clinic about it and get
rid of it. Modesty is a nice thing but not in such a case.

The notion that the habit of youth causes insanity is utter
nonsense. No capable doctor today believes it does. If it does,
most of the world would be insane, for few people pass the
years of youth without going through this habit.

I do not recommend the habit, for it is unhealthy, weakens
the body, fills one with gloom and lowers self-respect. But
if one gets into it there is not the slightest need of fearing insanity.

While it is true that the habit of youth is blamed for some
cases of insanity, the insanity did not come from the HABIT
but from the FEAR of it. Parents or somebody started the lie
that the habit would bring on insanity. Then the young folks
turned the fear round and round in their thought like a squir-
rel treading a cage until it upset their reason.

If you are suffering from this fear snap out of it, for there is
no sense in it at all. As long as the desire for sex is in our

thought it will have to be given some kind of relief. Most of us cannot overcome this desire until we get some other thought or habit or hobby to take its place. But the above prayer is the most powerful cure.

I will be criticized bitterly for writing these lines about the habit of youth in a book of this kind. However, if my advice will relieve suffering, I care nothing about the criticism of over-nice folks. Let them suffer through this hell as I did and they'll welcome my advice as a blessing sent from heaven.

The habit of youth and all badwill wants to be let alone in secret to eat the heart out of us all. I'm for bringing all badwill out into the light where it can be seen and killed.

And now something about the fear of dogs. Albert Payson Terhune, the great writer and lover of dogs, says in the *Reader's Digest* that we should not allow fear to master us when we are in the presence of an ill-tempered or peppery dog. For when we are frightened, nature pumps a lot of adrenalin into our blood. This throws off an odor which human nostrils do not smell. Dogs, however, smell it and hate it. It rouses some of them to rage. Many an otherwise gentle dog will attack when that odor reaches him.

Terhune also says the danger of getting hydrophobia from a dogbite is so small that we should have no fear of it at all. He also says that if a dog rushes at you, stand still and fold your hands across your chest so he will have nothing to take hold of. Then don't run. Back away slowly. But if we really love dogs we will have no fear of them and they will love us and come up to us wagging their tails.

The story is told of Jesus and Lazarus in a book now out of print. This book tells how they walked in the forest and serpents did not hiss at them and the wild animals came up to them to have their heads stroked.

If we let any fear into our thought we must suffer, for it poisons our body in the same way that irritation, anger, worry and all other kinds of badwill do. Fear throws our digestive organs out of order and hinders them from changing our food into blood.

When our food does not change properly into blood this is

called bad metabolism. Bad metabolism can cause many serious diseases. It may also cause high blood pressure which may lead to death. Is fear worth the price we must pay for the pleasure we get out of fear as a hobby? Fear and all badwill thoughts are slow self-murder.

When I can't kill fear any other way I say to myself, "All right, let the worst come. I don't care." If I say it and mean it the fear melts away. If I were only allowed to sing one song in life I would sing Eva Tangway's old vaudeville hit, "I don't care."

Suppose we did go insane and had to go to the "coocoo house!" What of it? There are worse places. A rich drunk who couldn't stop drinking placed himself in an insane asylum to see if they could break up his booze habit. When he got well he didn't want to leave because he liked the life so well.

Suppose we do lose our job or our business! Maybe it is a good thing, for perhaps we are trying to do work for which we have no talent. Maybe we are being awakened to see that we should take up some other kind of work.

As to our daily bread and butter, there is just one sure way to kill the ever-present fear that we will lose it. That one way is to do our work so well that our boss can't do without us. Or make our business give such fine service or such fine goods that customers will flock to us.

This is the only way we can be sure of an income in this world, as I explain later in the chapter on Success. If we give all we've got to our work with no thought of getting, this will always bring us an income.

The fear of sickness can be wiped out if we can understand why we get sick. We get sick because we owe a debt to the law of *Come-Back*. The suffering of sickness pays it off. It is just like paying off any debt. We should be happy and thankful that we are getting rid of that debt.

Or we can get rid of the sickness if we can change all our badwill thinking to Goodwill thinking. This is a hard thing to do all at once, as I have said. But no sickness can live in pure Goodwill thinking which takes us right into the presence of our Lord Jesus (God) who knows no such thing as sickness.

Maybe you say, "I am afraid the sickness may make me die." The way to stamp out the fear of death is to read the chapter on Death and the books it mentions.

The above ways of doctoring fear will help to ease us through our suffering from fear. But we will never get full freedom from fear until we break up the cause of fear.

"What is the cause of fear?" you ask. Fear is caused entirely by badwill thoughts of the 34 poisons. We send them out and have been sending them out all our lives. The poison of these badwill thoughts comes back to our body and scares us.

How simple this all is! If we send out thoughts of fear that we will lose our job or business they all come back and fill us with the terror of loss. Then our fleshly body is terror-stricken with the fear of loss.

But suppose we have sent out thoughts of harmony and prosperity. What would be coming back to us? Nothing but harmony and prosperity. Then we would be full of success and our body would have no fear of failure in it and, what is more, we would enjoy only harmony and success.

Suppose we send out badwill thoughts full of fear of sickness. Well, of course they come back and fill us with a panic about sickness and our fleshly body either feels sick or suffers from the terror of getting sick. We call this fear sickness or nervousness. But it is merely the return of the badwill thoughts of sickness which we sent out.

On the contrary, if we send out only thoughts of health, only thoughts of health will come back and we will not fear sickness. "As a man thinketh so is he." Which means as our soul willeth and thinketh so will our fleshly body behave.

We know in our heart that we have been sending out badwill thoughts of hate, anger, envy, resentment, worry, criticism, etc., all our lives. We know we shouldn't have sent them out. We know in our hearts that they are poisonous, badwill thoughts which will come back and poison us. We are afraid of these thoughts but don't know it. We are afraid of our wrongdoing.

These badwill thoughts have broken up our peace with our Lord Jesus (God). We feel it in our hearts but don't understand it. We can't get fully free from fear until we stop sending out badwill thoughts—thoughts of the 34 poisons—and send out only thoughts of Goodwill to everything and everybody.

But we can't stop badwill thoughts all alone by ourself. For badwill thoughts are from hell. They have all the power of hell in them. Only our Lord Jesus (God) has power over hell. Therefore, we should pray Him to help us overcome badwill thinking. Name the kinds of badwill you are resisting and ask His help. He always helps us, if we trust and wait patiently.

We will never get fully free from fear until we get at peace with Our Lord Jesus (God). And we will never feel at peace with Him until "the still small voice" inside of us whispers and says, "You have no badwill poisons in your heart."

CHAPTER 12

Selfishness

WHO could be a better person to write about selfishness than a man who has broken all the world's records for selfishness? That was I. Mine was not a money selfishness for I have always been rather loose with money. I had the worst kind of selfishness; namely, a self-love that wanted to keep my fleshly body always at ease and feeling fine.

I would go through hard, humdrum exercises every day to make my fleshly body feel good. I studied foods, followed diets, took deep breaths, watched my digestion, bowel movements and sleep with foolish care to keep my fleshly body always glowing with health.

The thought of how to keep myself feeling glorious was ever present. An Irish bricklayer said of me, "He must have a mighty valuable body. He takes such good care of it." "None I love so much as myself." That was I.

I never thought of the comfort of any other living soul—not even of my wife and children. I never liked other people and never wanted to be with them because their thought drew me away from thinking about the comfort of my "precious" body. I lived nearly 50 years in a town of 12,000 people without calling on more than 2 of my neighbors. Nobody ever came to our house except my wife's friends. I had no friends and didn't want any. They might disturb the seeming peace of my "precious" body.

I was the Levite who walked on the other side of the street if anyone needed help. This beastly selfishness was one of the main roots of all my sickness, fear, unhappiness and business trouble.

We cannot keep the fleshly body feeling good all the time, any more than we can always have sunshine, happiness and springtime. It will get out of order much of the time in spite of our fleshly striving to keep it healthy. Therefore my failure to keep it always feeling good built up a fear that my body was headed straight for sickness or death.

I was trying to live with ill will toward my fellows. Of course this sent out hate, envy, pride, resentment, selfishness and other poisonous badwill thoughts which all came home to roost. Their roosting in my bodily "coop" poisoned me with sickness, fear, unhappiness and failure.

What this selfishness did to my family, employees and everyone I met was vicious. I would sink them down into the depths of gloom with my selfish, badwill thought. My wife always had to do what I wanted to—never what she liked to do unless she went off and did it by herself. Even then she was miserable from the feeling that she was not doing enough for me.

My business employees didn't dare to say anything against my selfish notions. My wife, children and employees became unhappy servants to my self-love. When I would realize this at times it filled me with tears of sorrow but not with enough to make me change.

Riding on trains or ships or sleeping in hotels so upset the ease of my fleshly body that I either refused to do them or dragged my wife or sons along with me. I thought I needed them because of nervous fear but in reality I was selfishly trying to save my body from discomfort.

Many is the time I got my wife out of a sick bed to go with me on business trips. I really didn't need her. I could have gone alone but her presence eased my bodily discomfort. I thought I was afraid to go alone. But this was only a cloak to cover up the real cause—my selfish greed for ease.

This selfishness would say to me, "You need a vacation. It will be wonderful to go somewhere and get away from the city noise and troubles of business." My wife would pack for days, plans were made and the hope of a good time ran high. But when we got away my selfishness suddenly decided that it would be easier at home and we turned around and hurried back. Once we shipped our car and trunks to Florida and had them all sent back.

I called it nervous fear but it was only selfishness. No thought at all of the disappointment to my wife. No thankfulness for the fact that I had the money and the freedom with which to take a glorious vacation. There was only hard, miserable thinking about my "precious" body.

When I got home I longed to be back on the vacation. "Everybody (like me) wants to do what they can't, have what they haven't and be where they ain't." I was just a spoiled child grown up.

Thus my selfishness sought peace and got wretchedness. It often made me suffer so that I wept or thought of suicide. But one who has such an overdose of self-love is too cowardly to let his beloved body take a chance on the "journey from which no traveler returns."

What nonsense to think we can keep our "fleshly body" feeling healthy and happy when we are sending out poisonous greed for bodily comfort and other badwill thoughts every minute! They are bound to come back and flood us with misery.

One of the biggest reasons for all my suffering was fear and this fear was largely caused by my awful selfishness. I was always trying to save my body and keep it in the enjoyment of ease. That made me afraid of everything that might harm it and upset its peace. I was afraid a motor car might kill it or food might not digest and thus make the poor thing feel badly.

I was afraid I wouldn't get enough sleep, exercise, air and sunshine to keep my body in the selfish comfort I longed for. I was afraid my nerves would get out of whack and drive me insane. I was afraid my business would fail or I would lose my money. This, I thought, would plunge me into hell itself.

I was so selfish that I wanted to live forever with selfish comfort in the flesh and I feared that death would take that away from me. My fear came largely from my thinking only of myself and yet I did not know I was selfish except now and then when I got flashes of it. However, they were only flashes from which I sank back again into my old, hard selfishness.

But I did finally learn to let up on greed for selfish ease and put my thought on making life sweeter for other people. Then most all my fears and other troubles went away. And I found a glorious peace flooding through me that I never knew before.

My business could have grown far beyond what it did if my selfish pride of opinion had not shut out valuable ideas from employees and others. This also dampened the enthusiasm of the workers in my business. My selfishness also created enemies who "knocked" me and my business and thus hindered our success.

Furthermore, my selfishness drove many powerful friends away who could have helped my business. The more selfish one is, the less people want to buy goods from him. Everybody hates a selfish person. How true the Law of *Come-Back* is; namely, that whatever we give out comes back to us!

Selfishness like mine is so rotten nobody will live with it. It is a kind of mild insanity or old age. Nurses on such cases can't stand them more than a few months. Neurosis (which means a disease of the nerves) is merely selfishness.

Religions and nations bring hatred down on themselves by their own selfishness. There would be no religious strife, no wars, no dictators or anyone in want if selfishness could be taken out of every human heart.

I came down on the Merchants Limited train from Boston to New York one night. The passengers on this train were mostly business men—many of them "big shot" business men. I looked for a care-free face tender with unselfishness and love but found only faces full of greed, fear, gloom, worry, tightness and badwill. They were all slaves to the selfish greed for money.

Selfishness is a tight mode of thinking. We grab at money or fleshly comfort or whatever we want with a fierce grip. Few of us know what this does to our health. But it tightens up our fleshly organs so they cannot work naturally.

People complain that they cannot relax. Selfish thinking has a lot to do with it. For selfish thinking winds us up so tight we can't let loose and run down into relaxation.

The love of parents for their children is one of the worst

forms of selfishness. Some parents rule the every thought and act of their children. It is a rare case where a parent is willing for his child to use his own natural talent which God gave him to make a living with.

Do we not hear on all sides of the displeasure of the father when his son won't follow in the father's work? Do we not hear the grief of the parent because his child marries someone of his own personal choice rather than the choice of the parent?

The fond love of parents grows fonder as they grow older and the wants of old age begin to worry them. Some parents actually bring children into the world to support the parents.

I knew a woman who couldn't afford to give $5. to a charity but right afterward she spent $250. for a fur coat for herself. The selfishness of it never dawned on her. We should watch and work to see our selfishness as others see it.

There are more slaves in the world today than ever before. Millions are in concentration camps. In fact, all who live under a dictator are slaves. Except the bosses who live in luxury off of the labor of millions of slaves.

In Johannesburg, South Africa, I read about the gold mines. Down in them, 9,000 feet deep, black men slave in terrible heat, damp, thick air and sweat. They get 50¢ a day of 8 hours. Their eyes look sad and hopeless. They live in the most awful slums in the world full of disease, filth and perversion. All to make money for a few greedy hearts who don't need it!

What cruel selfishness that man is willing to fasten a life of slavery on his brothers just to gain a little ease and money for himself. Man is the worst beast on the face of the earth. Think of the white slavery in our own "civilized" country where it is a big, organized business.

Merchants and manufacturers in modern "educated" nations look with horror on this picture of slavery and yet the slavery they lay on their employees to make money which they don't need is only a little less beastly.

The owner of a large business ground down his helpless girl workers to starvation wages. They could only spend 10¢ a day for lunch. With the profits thus wrung from human misery the owner gave a fine art gallery to his city and was praised from the housetops as a great philanthropist! And what awful slaves men are who have to work in many factories and mines! The galley slaves of old suffered no worse than our slaves on production lines and all to satisfy the greed for money.

Selfishness has more to do with making people get married than love. The man wants to satisfy his appetite for sex; the woman, her lust for a meal ticket. Most of them don't know this. But down deep in their hearts unseen by them the urge of selfishness "ties the knot."

Business is a selfish desire for fame and fortune on the part of most big business men. Unselfishness would make them happier and more successful.

Why are we selfish? Because we think the money or the health we seek will bring ease and comfort to our bodies. But of course selfishness is one of the badwill poisons which bring back ONLY sickness, fear, and unhappiness.

How sad it is that we foolish mortals cannot understand that unselfishness instead of selfishness is the only road to health, happiness and success! Unselfishness sends out Goodwill thoughts of love, peace, mercy, health, kindness, service, etc. These all come back to bless the sender. Selfishness sends out vicious thoughts of badwill which all come back to poison and curse the sender.

A certain wealthy man never knew how to make gifts at Christmas time. One Christmas he handed a sum of money to a worker among the poor and asked her to give Christmas presents where they would do the most good.

She did and when the man read the letters of thanks from the receivers of his kindness he sat down and cried with happiness. He had never known before the joy that comes from unselfishness. He had known only the misery that comes from selfishness.

The giving done at Christmas time is a sad example of selfishness. We give to our family and children which is only selfish giving to those who neither need nor care for the gifts. Try cutting out the gifts at home for one Christmas and use the money to gladden the dreary homes of poverty where a merry

Christmas is like "angel visits few and far between." Few of us know that the cheer and charm of Santa Claus is wholly unknown to millions of children.

Let us go to these homes in person and give our gifts, instead of lazily giving to charity organizations. There we would see the poverty with our own eyes and the joy we have brought to sad hearts. That will make us forsake Christmas selfishness forever.

I know a doctor who runs a school for stutterers. The school never pays expenses but this unselfish soul pays the loss every year out of his small income. I never knew a man so happy as that doctor. He is giving relief to thousands of boys and girls bound by the terrible curse of stuttering. The happiness that comes back to him sticks out all over his face.

I know another man who earns $100,000 a year and gives it all away to help those who are suffering. Someone asked him why he saved nothing for a rainy day. He said he knew that what he was doing would come back to him and take care of him. "I can never stop giving for it brings me so much joy," he said. He understands the Law of *Come-Back*.

Here is a picture of our horrible selfishness written by Paul deKruif in the *Ladies' Home Journal*:

He tells of the slums lying low on the Ohio River where the poor people of Cincinnati live. Two slum workers named Marquette and Allen have been toiling there for years to help these suffering people.

He says: "Here in many a block nearly 200 people live jammed on 200 square feet of ground of our spacious America. Marquette says that the great bulk of these slum dwellers are honest, respectable people trying to give their children a chance to live.

"We stumbled up stairs whose dirtiness is hidden by darkness to the two-room home of a negro mother with 8 children. Her husband, hard working, earns $5 a week and no help from welfare. The winter sunlight comes pale through a clean little window onto 3 pickaninnies dressed in clean but ragged coats to keep them warm.

"Answering his mother's call, a 5 year old boy came in the door, rocking toward us on rickety legs. 'No, Ma'm. I can't get milk every day. If I has milk every other day I does well.' The mother had one quart of milk every other day for 8 children and yet dairy herds must be cut down because of too much milk!

"Now we walk into a 3 room 'home' of a white mother of 6 children. Five of them are with their mother crowded round a feeble cook stove in the one room that's heated at all. Flies hover around the face of the baby and crawl over its dirty, thin hands as it lies on a bed of rags." DeKruif says that the slums of all cities are like those of Cincinnati.

Paul deKruif's heart-breaking story should be read by every selfish person. He says that Marquette has been ready for years with practical and beautiful plans for rebuilding the slums of Cincinnati to hatch husky child life. But it would cost $150,-000,000. to build Marquette's city of sunshine and health and nobody wants to put up this large sum.

It's the same old story of selfishness. The wealthy will give little to relieve the suffering poor neighborhoods. The race must be uplifted by spending billions on higher education while multitudes must live a life of hell in rotten, stinking alleys of disease.

The names of the givers to education must glow on beautiful buildings and on the front pages of newspapers. A high place in society must be gained by these "splendid" gifts to the higher education which only 2% of our population can use. Pride must be satisfied while millions of children can have milk only every other day. And yet men of money wonder why they do not enjoy health and happiness!

Of course the wealthy say that the poor don't want modern apartments and would turn them into slums. This is only an excuse by which to forget their selfishness. But "They know not what they do." If they really understood how selfishness poisons their health and happiness they would spend ALL their money and time doing good for others.

The greatest unselfishness is to try and change the thinking habits of our fellowmen. If we could all be taught what I am trying to give out in this book our suffering from selfishness and other badwill thoughts would change to a sublime health and happiness we never knew before.

To give money to relieve misery is good and brings back blessings. But to show a man how to change from badwill to Goodwill thinking is the only good and lasting gift. For that gift fills a man with the power to change his whole life from sickness, gloom, fear and failure to health, happiness, fearlessness and daily needs. That is the greatest of all giving and it brings back to the giver a blessed bliss.

Want and war can never be wiped out until the hearts of men are changed from brutal selfishness to that kindly unselfishness which "loves his neighbor as himself." If man had an unselfish heart there would be no relief rolls and no wars.

United Nations, peace societies and meetings to get nations to lay down their arms are just a waste of time and money. War will never cease until the cause is killed. The cause is the demon of selfishness in the human heart.

But unselfish acts have got to be deeply unselfish with no thought of getting anything in return. For if they are done with the slightest idea of getting fame or thanks or anything at all out of them they bring back to us either nothing or the misery that always comes back from selfishness.

Overstreet, a psychologist, in his book entitled ABOUT OURSELVES says that illness is a strong belief that we have a certain disease. He says we build a tight fence around the belief that we have this disease and inside of that small fence we sit and think of nothing but our woe. What a perfect picture of how selfish thought holds us in sickness!

The more we think selfish thoughts, the more we think disease into our body. The more we think selfish thoughts, the more we think unhappiness into our heart. The more we think selfish thoughts, the more we think fear into our nerves. And the more we think selfish thoughts, the more we think failure into our business or job.

Try unselfishness, dear friends. You may be amazed to find

health coming into your body and fear fleeing from your
nerves. And I know you will find happiness flooding into your
heart and success coming back to you as a reward for your unselfish service to your customers or to your employer.

A selfish life is hell. It isn't worth living.

CHAPTER 13

Sin

SIN is love of ourself and love of the bad in the world. Love of ourself and the world connects us with hell. These two loves hook us up with hell just like a telephone connection can hook us up with a den of gangsters.

Over this wire of self-love and love of the world come all the 34 poisons from hell flooding into us. This direct wire brings the poisonous badwill thoughts of devils, satans, evil spirits and demons into our hearts.

This connection with hell is an open sewer through which all the 34 poison-gases of all the hells pour into our body. No wonder we are sick, unhappy and full of fear, worry, hard luck! All these torments come to us from love of self and love of the world, which flood us with the 34 poisons.

Few of us ever stopped to think that love of self and love of the world are rank poison. Jesus warned us of these poisons when He said, "Love not the world, nor the things of the world." And again when He said, "Love the Lord, thy God with all thy heart and with all thy soul, and with all thy mind. This is the first and great commandment. And the second is like unto it, Thou shalt love thy neighbor as thyself. On these two commandments hang all the law and the prophets.

THERE WOULD BE NO SICKNESS, UNHAPPINESS, FEAR, WORRY OR HARD LUCK IN THE WORLD IF LOVE OF SELF AND THE WORLD AND LOVE OF THE 34 POISONS DID NOT LIVE IN OUR HEARTS.

When we love ourself and love the world we are in hell right here and now. For our every act is swayed and managed by hell without our knowing it. Our minds and hearts are wide open to hell and closed to heaven.

Many of us know from reading the Bible that we must forsake love of self and love of the world. We know we should love only our Lord and the good in our brothers. So we join church and love our Lord Jesus (God) and our brothers part of the time, and hell (self and the world) most of the time. But this divided love won't get us anything.

"No man can serve two masters: for either he will hate the one, and love the other; or else he will hold to the one, and despise the other. Ye cannot serve God and mammon." This route won't lead us out of misery here or into heaven hereafter.

There is only one way to get rid of sin and that is to repent NOW—AT ONCE. Repentance means to change our heart from the love of self and the world to love of our Lord Jesus (God) and the good in our brothers. And of course to stop loving self and the world we have to stop loving the 34 poisons. For love of self and the world *is* love of the 34 poisons. We can't love our Lord and the good in our brothers as long as we love the 34 poisons and let them remain in us.

However, our Lord doesn't expect us to wipe out all the 34 poisons over night. That is a hard job and takes time. What our Lord wants us to do is to repent now while we are in the flesh. Repent now and start to turn our hearts away from love of self, love of the world and love of the 34 poisons. Repent now while in the flesh and begin to love ONLY Him and the good in our brothers.

When we do this He forgives all our sins and helps us all the way into heaven. He helps us in answer to our prayers. Helps us to lose all the 34 poisons. Helps us to lose all love of self and the world. He helps us because we can't make this big change in our heart all by ourself. We must pray for His help.

We have to grow out of the badwill love of self and the world. We have to grow into love of our Lord and the good in our brothers. We keep growing out of badwill into Goodwill throughout eternity. Even the angels in heaven have to grow into more and more purity. This growing is called regeneration·

But, dear friends, repent and start to change now—at once. Don't wait and try to do it after death.

The author of THE GOLDEN FOUNTAIN says, "Oh how can I convey any warning of this terrible knowledge (of waiting until after death to repent)! Soul! Repent and return (to love of our Lord and our brothers) while still in the (fleshly) body." Swedenborg cries out this alarm all through his 30 books. And Jesus said, "Except ye repent, ye shall all likewise perish."

Listen to it, dear friends, and repent now while there is yet time. Start today on the joyous golden path to heaven.

CHAPTER 14

Happiness

WHY do people drink whiskey or take dope? For pleasure, you say. No, that isn't the real reason. They do it to forget the miseries of life for a few short moments.

Why do people drink coffee and tea? Why do they play golf and cards? Why do they gamble and go in for other so-called pleasures? Because it gives short relief from the sufferings of life.

What are the woes of life? We call them sickness, failure, sorrow, hard work, disappointment, bad luck, poverty and what not. To most of us there seems no freedom from these miseries except a few moments of rest in strong drink or in a few hours of so-called pleasure.

But we can't get drunk with liquor or dope or pleasure and thus gain relief from the unhappiness of life except for a little while. Such relief is short-lived and lands us right back in misery where we started.

However, there is a way out of the woes of life if we are willing to change our thinking. We must first be willing to learn that the heartaches of life do not come from failure, sorrow, hard work or from anything outside of us. No thing outside of us makes us wretched.

The unhappiness of life comes from inside of us—from our own wrong thinking. We don't know how to think right. We think ourselves into sickness and trouble without knowing it and then blame it on something outside of us, such as wrong kind of food, germs, bad luck, loss of money and the acts of other people.

We think bad thoughts most of the time. We think them

without knowing we do. Two-thirds of the adjectives in the dictionary are bad thoughts. This proves that our thoughts are mostly bad. Bad thoughts poison us—make us sick— make us afraid—make us fail—make us unhappy.

We fill our thinking full of black, badwill thoughts (with the 34 poisons) such as hate, anger, fear, worry, envy, resentment, criticism, selfishness, etc. We send out these bad thoughts. They come back and bring sickness, failure and unhappiness into our lives without our knowing it. Then we try to drown these woes in strong drink, dope or pleasure. But they won't drown.

We go to all sorts of lengths to keep our fleshly bodies fit. But we never give the slightest thought to keeping our thoughts healthy. And yet the kind of thinking we do swings our life to the left in misery or to the right in happiness.

We can never be happy until we stop sending out badwill thoughts. For they all return to us in accordance with the Law of *Come-Back* and poison us with a life of gloom and sorrow.

If we would stop only a part of our badwill thoughts the power of Goodwill thinking would flood us with much peace, health, happiness and with many of our daily needs. For its power is so great that only a little of it brings a beautiful calm and peace into our hearts. If you don't believe it, try it.

Freedom from care, fear, worry and want is really the happiness we seek. How easily they may be gained by stopping badwill. For this would allow the divine happiness of the Holy Spirit to flow out of our hearts into our whole body and life.

Emmet Fox writes beautifully of the Arabs: "Free from the care of property to defend, they live a simple, wandering life that breeds health, happiness and their daily needs. Filled with the sheer joy of living, one of them looked out from his tent at the myriad stars and said, 'The desert is the Garden of Allah.' " So free was he from mean, badwill thoughts that even the desert looked to him like the Garden of God.

What a picture of peace within! How different from the modern "badwillers" in the streets of our great cities, rushing willynilly with their faces full of fear—fighting for money— fighting off disease—fighting for false, fleeting pleasures that turn into misery—fighting to keep off the wolf—dreading always the unsafety of life!

We can never be happy until we give up all selfish desire. Desire for fame, fortune, power, liquor, tobacco—desire for too much food and too much sex—all selfish desires are the cause of all unhappiness. We can't get everything we want and that makes us unhappy.

Selfish desire can never be satisfied. The more we get of any selfish desire, the more we want of it. This makes us always miserable. We should desire only health and our daily needs and know that they will be supplied as long as we are on earth. For our loving Lord Jesus takes care of us just the same as He takes care of the stars.

At first we may fight against this idea of having no selfish desire. But just stop and think how joyously happy we would be if we had no desire to make us slave all our lives to get it satisfied. We'd be free and freedom of the heart and thought is happiness.

We can never be happy in the slavery we go through to get fame, fortune, power, booze, nicotine, piles of food, too much sex, luxurious homes, riches, etc. "Selfish desire makes slaves of us all." Chasing the selfish desires of life is "Paradise Lost."

However, not all desires make us miserable. There are 2 unselfish desires that give us blissful happiness. One is the desire to help others and forget ourselves. The other is the desire to blast out badwill and fill our thinking with nothing but Goodwill. Trying to satisfy these 2 unselfish desires is "Paradise Regained."

"Badwillers" can never be happy until they stop badwill thoughts and surrender themselves to our peacegiving and beloved Lord Jesus. Civilization can never make man happy, for civilization is built on badwill and badwill is the bitter enemy of happiness.

Perhaps you doubt that the stopping of badwill can make you happy. Well, let me ask you—if we hate somebody, which is a badwill thought, does that make us happy? No; it fills us with misery, for our hate echoes back and poisons us. But what comes back to us when we feel a genuine sense of Goodwill toward others?

If we get irritated or angry, which is badwill thinking, does that make us happy? No; our anger shatters our nerves and upsets the adrenal glands. Over-excitement in these glands hinders our digestion. This causes indigestion, biliousness and constipation which may bring on other serious diseases.

If we criticize our brother we can feel our bad criticism coming back and filling us with a sad heart. Does that make us happy? No! But if we give out Goodwill to our brother we can feel the glow of our Goodwill returning to us.

If we are selfish and greedy, people hate us and run from us. Does that make us happy? No! But if we give our lives to helping other people we feel the greatest joy in life coming back to comfort us. There is no joy like the joy of sinking selfishness and doing for others.

Indeed, is it not "more blessed to give than to receive"? To receive great wealth is to receive care, worry, fear of loss, slavery to money, misery aplenty. Wealthy people are nearly always unhappy. Wealth carries the curse of unhappiness with it. It is the curse of America. But to give out Goodwill and help to others brings peace, contentment, joy—brings back what we gave out.

Goldsmith sang of "the luxury of doing good." And from Milton we read, "happy in mutual help." What beautiful, joyous thoughts!

Whenever we are unhappy it is a sign that we are not giving out enough. Selfishness is getting the better of us. That's the time when we should get on the job and see if we can help someone who is suffering from sickness, need, fear or unhappiness. Then our misery will change to joy.

One of the chief causes of unhappiness is not giving thanks for anything. Most of us are not thankful for what we have in the way of health, daily needs and happiness. We are always longing for something we haven't and forgetting to be thankful for what we have. I have written a whole chapter on how Thankful Thought Heals.

And what of jealousy, another kind of badwill thinking? I used to be jealous of everyone who was more successful than I. Everybody preached at me to stop it. But preaching only makes us fight against the preaching. However, I learned that if I sent out thoughts of jealousy they would come back and make me unhappy.

I saw the price I was paying for being jealous, as I have said. Then I stopped it and I cannot tell you what a load it lifted from me. Instead of being jealous of others I learned to be glad for everybody's success and deeply thankful for whatever success I had however little it might be. Try this and see what peace and happiness it will bring.

And what of resentment and revenge? I was always full of these nasty, badwill thoughts. If anybody did anything harmful to me I either resented it fiercely or "got even." I learned that if I kept on resenting and getting revenge for wrongs done me I must suffer from unhappiness. Therefore, not wanting to be unhappy from the comeback of my thoughts of resentment, I trained myself gradually to try to return Goodwill for wrongs. I can never tell you what a load of unhappiness that lifted off me.

Pride is another cause of bitter unhappiness. "Pride goeth before a fall." It surely does! We who are proud want to rise to the fame of Napoleon or the riches of Rockefeller or the proud pedestal of a movie star. Few of us vain jackasses can reach such heights. When we don't we descend into the depths of hellish unhappiness. Finally I saw that pride is an unsatisfiable desire. So I said, "To the dogs with pride—I'll none of it." That brought me a new and glorious feeling of freedom and happiness.

And so on down the line of badwill thoughts. They are all poison—all killers of happiness. The whole cause of unhappiness is badwill.

People who have the most trouble with sickness and poverty are happier than we who have health and success. I passed a man without legs on a crowded street. He was sitting in one of those tiny trucks on rollers which legless men use, pushing himself along with his hands on the sidewalk. He was whistling, while I had a sober face full of worry lest I would not have a good bowel movement that morning!

Those who try to find happiness in the pleasures of life, such as cocktail parties, dinners, dances, cards, movies, etc., are doomed to misery. These flimsy pleasures do not give happiness. They only give empty pleasures which melt quickly into misery because the desire for pleasure can never be satisfied. If I wanted to live the emptiest life that the world can give I would chase these rainbows of pleasure.

Happiness is made of deeper stuff. Happiness comes from stopping badwill and giving the happy power of Goodwill the right of way through us. Pain and pleasure come and go. But the real happiness of life comes from "the way our heart feels inside of us." "The kingdom of heaven is within you."

The so-called pleasures of life never satisfied me for they always came to an end too soon. If I went to a ball game the ninth inning came too quickly. If I enjoyed a play the last curtain made me sad.

If a few drinks boosted me up I dreaded the letdown and return to the dumbness of life. No pleasures bought from the outside seemed to satisfy me. They all picked me up for a little while and then let me down into the same old, drab humdrum of life.

But when I found that the stopping of badwill, even in part, filled me with peace, I knew at last I had won my hunt for happiness. I had at last found the way to a satisfying enjoyment that didn't wear out.

I had found that happiness comes from the purity of our thinking and from a pure heart within and not from any pleasure or anything we can buy from the outside. I had learned that eating, drinking, smoking and all pleasures gotten from the outside are the flimsy, foolish "heaven" of the badwill man. I had learned that this "heaven" is always cracking up and letting man down into an everpresent hell.

And I had learned that if man is willing to stop his badwill thinking he can live in a divine flow of health, plenty and happiness. For they flood through him naturally when he gives them a chance. Mrs. Eddy said, "Outside of personal sense all is harmony." My way of saying the same thing is, "Outside of badwill all is health, success and happiness."

My wife never knew much unhappiness because she never leaned on outside pleasures for enjoyment. She is happy from within—always thankful for what she has—always happy within no matter what outside troubles she has to face. On the other hand, I was always miserable because I tried to get my happiness from outside pleasures.

You probably think that nobody can overcome all of his badwill thoughts. You will probably argue that if anyone could do so he would be an angel. We may not be able to overcome them all in this life. But each time we get the best of one of them, even in part, we let in more of the happy light of Goodwill which gives us a grand uplift.

To win the victory over badwill is all that's worth fighting for in this life. All other victories will fail to give us happiness. To win success in education, science, art, money, power, etc., is as nothing when set along side of the happiness that comes from the overcoming of badwill.

The most interesting thing in the world is the study of human nature—especially the study of one's self. What greater victory—what greater joy—than to have overcome every badwill thought!

Alexander brought the whole world to his feet. Then mourned for more worlds to crush. But we who stamp out our badwill shall wish for no more worlds to conquer, for we have gained peace, plenty, joy, happiness forever.

More than these no man can want, for they are his lifelong desire even though he may not understand now that they are. He who overcomes his badwill is a greater hero than all the heroes of all the battles of all kinds ever fought. That is why Jesus was the greatest hero of mankind.

Another builder of happiness for me was learning the habit of taking everything cheerfully that comes to pass, no matter what it may be. All my life I wanted to reform everything and everybody (that is, make them all over for the better).

Finally I found that reformers don't reform much, if anything. I found that reforms come only when people can stand themselves and their lives no longer. Everything in life is unfolding like a flower unfolds in obedience to the plan of our Lord Jesus (God). It is going to work out in accordance with this plan and I found that I might as well let reforms alone and be happy.

We should know that everything that happens is for our good, for it is His Will. If we can really have faith in that great Truth it will wipe out oceans of misery and bring in a peaceful sea of happiness.

One night as I listened to a beautiful piece of music by a great orchestra, this thought came to me:

Where does the tenderness and melody of music and poetry come from? They come from the Goodwill and love of our Lord Jesus (God). They could never come from the black, fighting meanness of badwill. Therefore, if we could stop our badwill we would be flooded always with tenderness, melody, love, beauty and happiness.

One thing in my makeup has always given me great happiness. That one thing is the love of doing something fine just for the love of doing it fine. Without this I could never have stood the many sufferings I have gone through.

The joy that comes from a job well done is one of the big thrills of life. The greatest "kick" I have always gotten out of my business was not that of making money. It came from making our goods as fine as I could make them. A passion for perfection brings great happiness.

In writing this book I am trying with all my might to write it with such simplicity and clearness that everyone may read it and understand easily the workings of our thought. Maybe I am not succeeding but the feeling that I am giving all that I have to the work fills me with happiness.

What must have been the joy of men like Shakespeare, Richard Wagner, Michael Angelo and Thomas Edison who longed to do something better than it had ever been done before! Or even of Bartlett Arkell who found joy in making the finest bacon and chewing gum that he could make!

Elbert Hubbard said, "If your job is that of a barber, be the finest barber in the world. If a waiter, be the finest waiter in the world." We can find sweet happiness in a job well done however lowly the job may be.

We all know the saying "Life is just what we make it." We ourselves make it miserable or happy. Nobody and no thing makes us miserable or happy but we ourselves. "We have made ourselves just what we are. We are just what we have thought."

I always had a good home. I deeply enjoyed the home of my childhood and youth. But during most of my 53 years of married life I never took much interest in my home as a family man, despite the fact that my wife has always been a splendid homemaker. I sought pleasure from the outside.

But what a mistake! During the last few years I have seen the joy one can get out of a home. I built myself a pine room with an old pot stove in it. How many happy hours I have spent there in writing and in looking out through the 7 colonial windows into my wife's beautiful garden! I have even learned to like the garden, the trees, the birds and the neighborhood and our town in which I had never taken any interest before.

And wonder of wonders for me, I am learning to enjoy the reading of books! All my life I hated to read. My silly pride made me believe that nobody knew how to write. The joy of reading can bring us a paradise of endless happiness. Now, instead of wasting my time reading newspapers too thoroughly and going to movies I read useful books.

Magazines, newspapers, radio, and television and movies are shallow things to waste much precious time on. A fine book is the outpouring of a great thought or a great experience of some great man or woman told by them in their most brilliant moments. To travel with them through their magnificent thoughts and experiences fills me with priceless knowledge and great happiness.

This useful reading gives me business ideas that are highly profitable. Furthermore, the knowledge we store up from good reading gives a charm to our talk that brings much happiness. The more I read of great books, the more I lose interest in news, movies, radio and television. You, too, will change to the higher, satisfying happiness as you wipe out more and more badwill.

It is just as vital to keep poison pictures and the poison of bad thoughts out of one's thinking as it is to keep poison out of the stomach. I will not allow anything but happy music, happy reading or happy thinking to enter into me if I can help it.

Newspapers make all bad news look worse than it is. They have to make news sound awful to get us to read it. This drags us down and fills us with a load of gloom. Don't believe all the bad news in the newspapers for it isn't half as bad as they picture it. Much of it is poisonous propaganda put out by nations and selfish organizations.

Charles W. Ferguson in the *Southwest Review* says that he is a happy man who has simplified his tastes to the point where a good book and a fire and a quiet evening can give him sublime happiness.

Happiness comes only from stopping badwill. Then the heavenly harmony rolls in like a tidal wave. Poets and composers feel this divine harmony at moments when they write masterpieces. They could not imagine their wonderful outbursts of beauty.

We know the joyous thoughts we have when listening to a piece of music we like. We could have these happy thoughts always if we would keep badwill out and stick to Goodwill thinking. And how that joyous thinking would breathe health, success and happiness into our hearts!

"Every good thought is a flower and every bad thought a thorn." "Happy thoughts and cheerful ways make happy days." But alas, "Unhappiness is sweet to some of us" like Juliet who said, "Parting is such sweet sorrow," and like Louise whose friends said of her, "Poor Louise, so unhappy and so eager to share it." Unhappiness is a kind of thinking which has wandered away from Goodwill. It has strayed away into the darkness of badwill thoughts.

We should never be unhappy because we can't make a lot of money. For money-making is a gift. A few people like

Croesus and Rockefeller had it. Most of us haven't it. So let's not waste our life trying to do something we have no talent for. Besides, the money won't give us happiness even if we make it, for it builds up mountains of care. The nearer we can get to having no desire for the things of this world, the nearer we will come to happiness.

Whenever we feel sour and grouchy we should think of Abraham Steinberg who is only a dooropener (guard) in a dirty, noisy, gloomy subway train in New York. Yet he is one of the happiest men alive. The *New Yorker* wrote him up and quotes some of his station calls as follows:

"Here we are at good old 96th Street, folks." "Step along, folks, and we'll get you downtown in time for work." "Take your time, madam" (speaking to a woman with a baby), "I will hold these restless portals." "Why here's good old Lots Avenue, people! Last stop! Thank you and hope to see you again." We can be happy in any job or place in life if we want to be.

A blind boy said, "I feel and hear things which people who see don't. Therefore I feel compensated (paid) for being blind." Let me say it again—anyone can be happy who wants to be. Unhappy people don't want to be happy. They enjoy "sweet heartache" and sour gloom.

When Thoreau, ill with TB, could wander no more among his beloved woods and creeks and lakes and flowers and had to stay indoors, he said, "I enjoy life as much as ever." This proves to me that the Holy Spirit inside of us is always happy without any outside entertainment and would make us always happy if we would get our badwill out of its way.

I know a blind man 80 years old who has lived happily in his room with his radio and dog for 10 years. This proves again that happiness is a thing of the heart and does not come from outside entertainment.

Somebody said, "What a soothing relief to get stewed and be free from the 'wonders' of civilization." But such freedom is only for a few moments. The only lasting and satisfying freedom from the miseries of life is to blot out badwill thinking.

I know a little island where peace reigns. The people are

simple-thinking souls. They live a home life in beautiful, old colonial houses which have not been changed. The town is a perfect picture of colonial days.

All the rush and crash and greed and hard-heartedness of the city are missing. Nobody ever locks a door. The thought there is kind, soothing, restful. It is a Goodwill thought. What happiness such thought would bring to us all if it were everywhere!

I always try to remember a lot of foolish (not filthy) stories and tell them whenever I can get an audience. They get a laugh all around and these laughs take poison out of us. Lincoln was always full of stories. He would stop the affairs of state any time to tell a story that happened to come to him.

We must admit that to think good thoughts makes us feel good; whereas the thinking of bad thoughts makes us feel bad.

Therefore what is to be gained by thinking bad thoughts? What is there to be gained by hanging on to bad thinking? By thinking good and holding fast to good thoughts I have been able to lift, soothe and heal myself. So as for me, I will ever try to think only good.

A friend of mine got tired of the noise and misery of life and thought he'd try some quiet way to find happiness. So he went to a Quaker Church. For two solid hours no word was spoken. At first he said the silent peace was painful because he was so used to noise. But gradually the silence began to soothe him.

After the meeting he said, "I felt full of a beautiful peace in my thought and heart all day." How this modern world does need to know that happiness is right inside of our heart in the Holy Spirit that lives there. But we won't let it work for us! We think we have to run outside of ourselves and do something to be happy.

The heaviness we feel on a spring day or a warm day or on a "blue Monday" is not the heaviness of body. It is heaviness of thinking. Our body weighs the same, whether we feel blue or light-hearted. The heaviness comes from badwill thinking. If we change to Goodwill thinking the heaviness will go away and, lest we forget, let me repeat WE CAN CHANGE.

Goodwill thinking is like sunshine. Sunshine comes in and

gladdens every nook and corner of our house if we let it. So Goodwill thinking floods every nook and corner of our body with health, daily needs and happiness if we stop our badwill thinking and let it in.

Our Lord Jesus (God) runs this big universe in beautiful harmony. Nothing in it ever gets out of order. We are just as much a fixed part of the universe as the stars and the sun. Therefore the Holy Spirit of our Lord Jesus, working in our heart, will run us always in harmony if we will get our badwill out of the way.

Perhaps you say that the universe does not always run in harmony. Perhaps you say, "Look at the earthquakes, clouds, storms, tidal waves, etc.!" But the smooth-working universe takes no notice of them. The universe moves on in spite of them. They are caused like all bad things by the badwill thinking of man. When enough of man's badwill gathers together in one place it blows up in what looks like an earthquake, storm, etc.

A beautiful church service or the silence of the desert or looking at the sky as we lie on the ground frees us for a while from the ocean of badwill thinking in life. It is a tiny taste of the natural harmony of the Holy Spirit in our heart. Why not stamp out badwill thoughts and thus hold ourselves always in this bliss and happiness of the Holy Spirit?

Only our own poisonous, badwill thinking keeps divine bliss from bubbling out of every pore and filling us with heavenly happiness. This bliss is the silver lining of the clouds. The dark side of the cloud is our badwill. But the silver lining of bliss is always there.

"Life is worth living while we are giving moments of paradise to others." "The greatest thing in life is happy thoughts. The art of life is to have as many of them as possible."

Think of the Chinese. They are satisfied with a full stomach. If they get anything else they call it luxury (high living). They get joy out of growing a single flower or out of looking at a single picture. If they get no luxury they are still happy. But we slave all our lives to get luxuries that give us no peace!

Whenever I am full of happiness my fleshly training rises up inside of me and says it isn't right to have all this peace. It won't last. However, happiness is our divine right. It belongs to us. But most of us won't take it and enjoy it.

Freedom is the great giver of happiness. We live in "the land of the free and the home of the brave." Therefore we think we are free. That kind of freedom is good but it is only a tiny part of freedom.

The real freedom that fills us with happiness is freedom from care, worry, fear, hate, anger, envy, jealousy. Freedom from resentment, revenge, pride, selfishness, irritation, gloom, want, disease. Freedom from bad habits and the overdoing of appetites. Freedom from criticism of others. Freedom from being bossed by the family. Freedom from slavery to business and money. Freedom from a bored life. Freedom from all the 34 badwill poisons. Freedom from everything except that which makes our heart feel finer. All this happy freedom would be ours if we would get rid of badwill thinking.

Gaining freedom from bad habits has given me the most blessed peace. To be chained to bad habits is slavery. I always feel sad when I see a young person falling innocently under a bad habit. For it is so easy to slip into a bad habit and so hard to break its steel grip. If young people could only see the slavery and misery of bad habits they would never start them. What a life full of hell this would save them!

I asked a doctor why he did not smoke and drink and overeat. He said, "I don't want to go through the misery they make me suffer afterward."

But you say, "How can we stop a bad habit?" By learning to know that there is no pleasure in it. And by praying to Our Lord Jesus to help us stop it. See our pamphlet entitled: "HOW TO LOSE ALL LOVE FOR LIQUOR AND TO-BACCO." There really is no joy in a bad habit. For every ounce of seeming pleasure in a bad habit we pay tons of misery. When we give up the seeming pleasure of a bad habit a new joy of purity takes the place of it. I have found this to be absolutely true. "Where the spirit (purity) of the Lord is, there is liberty."

When we give up a bad habit we don't give up any *thing*.

We lay down a heavy burden and enter into the joy of higher self-respect and victory over the beast in us. Our heart feels finer and that is a blessed reward. We feel a new happiness of purity in our heart that pays us many times over for dumping out the bad habit.

To gain sweet freedom from the badwill slaveries of life is the real freedom and happiness of life. This freedom breeds in our heart a peace and love and happiness that is nothing short of paradise. And we can ALL have this free, happy heart if we are WILLING to give up our badwill. One thing is certain: We will never gain happiness until we gain freedom from badwill.

"The goal of every soul is freedom." We are all striving for freedom in every thought and act of our life and don't know it. Our very longing for freedom and our life-long battle to get it proves that there is a glorious freedom for us all.

Throughout my life I have thought I would like to live the life of a small farmer. While the work would be hard and the hours long, still I would have more freedom—freedom from the heavy yoke of business—freedom from the hurly-burly of the city—freedom to sit in the silence of the woods at times and read and doctor my thought.

Many there be who howl that you can't make a living on a farm. But through all the many hard times in the history of our country the thrifty farmers of New England have made a good living in spite of their rocky soil and with little help from the Government. It's all a matter of being willing to work and save.

Thinking the thoughts of badwill imprisons us in a life of black, stormy night. By forsaking them we open up our heart and the beautiful thoughts of Goodwill from the Holy Spirit in our heart come shining all through us.

Then we find ourselves bathing in the soft sunshine of heavenly June. We "walk beside the still waters and lie down in green pastures" and enjoy "the peace that passeth all (badwill) understanding."

But as long as we know in our heart that we are guilty of wrongdoing we can never be happy. Hate is wrongdoing—

bad criticism is wrongdoing—all badwill is wrong doing,
wrong thinking that strikes back and poisons us. Happiness is
freedom from badwill—freedom from the 34 badwill poisons.
The freer we are from badwill, the happier we are. There is no
other happiness.

CHAPTER 15

Resistance

YOU have probably been resisting (fighting against) every-thing I have said in this book. You are doubtless saying to yourself, "What nonsense to claim that all we need do to have health, happiness and daily needs is to stop the 34 poisonous badwill thoughts. Then change over to Goodwill thinking. Nice theory but it won't work."

This doubt is aflame in all of us. But it really isn't doubt. It is resistance. We don't want to give in to what another person says. Most of us are full of stubborn, contrary, cussed resist-ance. Our thought is closed. We don't want to agree with any-body. We don't like to give in to what another person says. "The hardest thing to give is—in." We want to take the other side. We like to resist.

This hard, mulish side of us makes us resist everything which anybody brings up about anything. Especially about such ten-der thoughts as love and Goodwill which are so gentle and un-like our harsh, beastly nature. A child still in the innocent sweetness of early childhood does not resist. But the cast-iron heart of man soaked in badwill resists everything.

Besides, we like to stick to our badwill thoughts. We like to drag our thought down into the sewer and drink booze and swear and smoke and hog up food and tell dirty stories and make swine out of ourselves.

We don't want to rise up into the sweetness of gentle love, peace and noble, Goodwill thinking. We don't want to let go of these badwill, gutter thoughts until they come back and torture us with suffering. Then only are we willing to humble ourselves and change to Goodwill thinking.

But our worst resistance boils up when we hear the truth about what we are. Just let someone try to make us believe that sickness, fear, unhappiness, failure and death come from our thinking, and not from our flesh! Then our childhood education rises up like an active volcano and belches out bitter resistance. For we don't want that proud education tumbled down into the ditch.

All down through the ages men have resisted the Truth; namely, that all things come from thought and not from flesh. Witness the resistance to this Truth as taught by Jesus. This resistance brought violent death to all His disciples except John and to Jesus himself. We don't want to know the Truth about ourselves even though it would free us from all the woes of life.

How we punish ourselves by resisting! We fight and fight and fight in every way possible to keep badwill in and Goodwill out—to keep sickness in and health out—to keep unhappiness in and joy out—to keep failure in and success out. Oh, how we suffer from this stubbornness without knowing it!

After we have suffered until we can't stand it any longer, we yield and grow meek and childlike if our stubborn badwill hasn't killed us. We surrender humbly and give ourselves up to Goodwill thinking. Then the power of Goodwill rushes in and frees us from our misery. And oh how sweet is this freedom from our headstrong cussedness! With what ease we could have broken away from our trouble if we had just been willing to give up our resistance and let Goodwill thinking do its blessed work!

We have already proved that it is unsafe to have any faith in flesh and matter. Yet we let our belief in their power keep right on selling us the lie that bad is true and good is only true part of the time. We keep right on letting this belief tell us that sickness, unhappiness and failure are more likely to come to us than health, happiness and success.

We long for harmony and prosperity—oh how we long for them! And yet we resist to the last ditch the simple truth about the workings of our thinking and our bodies which would bring us these joys. Even in the midst of hard suffering most of us will resist the loving power of Goodwill thinking, ever eager to help us through our misery.

Still more unbelievable is the fact that after we have gotten through a hard spell of sickness or trouble by doctoring our thought we still resist. Often we do not see our resistance. We may claim that we do not resist. We may think that we love the truth about ourselves and want it.

But when we try to read and work to change our thought over to Goodwill thinking, what happens? A silent argument from our old, fleshly education tells us we haven't time or we must attend to some other work or we are too tired, etc. Cunning excuses come thick and fast into our thought to keep us from learning more of the truth and from gaining more faith in it.

"Talking serpents" from hell rise up in us. They bring up the remembrance of our wrong education. They rise up in our thought from the past and tell us to believe in the power of flesh and matter.

Resistance is the kind of badwill that makes us unwilling to give up badwill. It is resistance more than any other kind of badwill that holds us in sickness, fear, unhappiness and failure.

Whenever we get a childlike willingness to give up our resistance we will see a big change for the better in our health, happiness, fear and prosperity. But the tearing down of resistance is a hard job with some of us. For resistance is like a weed. We can cut it down but it will grow right up again in our thought. We must dig resistance up by the roots and be sure the roots are ALL out.

Resistance to a disease or any trouble is dangerous. For it builds up another disease or trouble of the same kind which comes back and makes us suffer from another dose of the same torment.

My first practitioner used to say, "Why don't you drop it?" meaning, "Why do you hang on to your disease or trouble? Why not 'loose it and let it go?'" But I had too much resistance. I just stubbornly resisted the thought of letting go of my sickness or misery and of course they just stayed with me.

We only need one kind of badwill in our thought to keep us sick, unhappy, fearful or a failure. "For whosoever shall keep the whole law and yet offend in one point, he is guilty of all."

Strange to say, I resisted writing this book. My resistance was always telling me that the writing of this book was an awful job, full of tedious, hard work. It also argued to me that nobody would read it anyway. My resistance always got in the way and tried to keep me from finishing this book.

Here is a very simple way to break down resistance. It is so simple that we won't think it amounts to much at first. But after we try it we will be astonished at its power.

The way to break down resistance is to say "I AM WILLING." Think it! Feel it! Say it! "I am willing to let go—let loose of my resistance. I am willing to see that I can never be healed until I am willing to stop resisting the power of Goodwill thinking."

We must say to ourselves, "I am willing," over and over again without end until the resistance is broken. But merely speaking these words will do no good. We've got to really let go of resistance and be honestly and humbly willing in our heart to let go of it.

"Except ye become as little children, ye shall not enter into the kingdom of heaven." Get into that mellowness of thought and resistance will thaw out, melt down and flow away.

We should also use our war cry IT CAN CHANGE. For resistance CAN CHANGE over to a full surrender to the power of Goodwill thinking if our heart is honestly willing to let it change. Unless we are willing to change there is no good in trying to heal by changing our thought. If we are not willing to change then we are doomed to sit in our resistance until badwill kills us.

Many of us will resist doctoring our thought and then go around in the "backyard" and try to be willing to change and take it up. But this is not being willing. We've got to give up our resistance openly and aboveboard and soften into love and gentleness and Goodwill to all.

If we find it hard to overcome resistance just keep on trying

day by day to break it down and keep praying to our Lord
Jesus (God) to help us. It will grow less and less as we see the
wonderful changes in our body and our life that come to us
from being willing.

CHAPTER 16

Success

MY FATHER could have "gone places" in the business world but was held back by the need of making a living for a large family. Therefore he could not take a chance on building up his own business. He had to stick to the safety of his salary.

My mother had a burning desire for money success. She resented my father's fear about quitting his job and going into business for himself to make a fortune. She would say, "If I were only a man I could do something."

Thus I was brought up under the ever-present wail that we were not rich. Naturally I grew up to believe that life was not worth living unless I could make a fortune in order that I might retire (get away) from the misery of the world some day and take mine ease.

So I began my business life at 23 with jaws set to win money at any cost. For 46 years I turned myself into a boiling volcano of fear, worry, anger, irritation, envy, greed, hatred, resentment and all the other badwill thoughts. And for what? To grab money.

Every waking hour was slavishly given over to making money. I got into business for myself at 28. For 43 years I gave everything I had to that business. It was a terrible drive of badwill to pile up money. The business world would call me a success.

Now, after 46 years in the battle of business, I could retire at the age of 77. But strange to say I have no desire to retire! I find that nothing could be more dull than dumb ease from which all the "kick" of life has flown. I find that to retire is to shut the door on all the thrilling interest of life and thus let my lively thinking of a lifetime run down and die.

I find that money can buy beautiful houses but we tire of them for they are just houses—not homes. I find that money can buy food, liquor and sex in quantity but their very quantity dulls the appetite for them. I can buy many of the costly pleasures of modern life but their charm soon fades.

I can give money to charity but having been so full of greed for 46 years I give away only what I don't want. Such giving brings small comfort because the giving is not from the heart. I can buy false, fleeting friends who are only friendly to the little money I have. I can buy position in society but that is an empty honor. I can buy doctors to comfort my fear and lawyers to keep me out of trouble. Yes, I can buy most anything but what comfort does it give me?

Moreover, I find money, property and business cares enslave me in an endless strain to hold on to them, for money is easier to get than to keep. There can be no peace where there is strain. "Uneasy lies the head that wears a crown" of money. And my very "success" has built up envy, jealousy and hatred toward me. As my second teacher said, "We are madly trying to get money at any price. The result will be empty."

Charles Schwab, the steel king, when sailing for Europe at the age of 75, said he was sorry that he had given his life entirely to money-making because it brought him too much power. Mr. Schwab doubtless meant that money-making had failed to satisfy.

I feel worse about it than Mr. Schwab. To me the saddest regret of my life is the fact that I have given nearly all of it to business. This has always been against my nature. I have always felt a burning desire inside of me to spread beauty and sweetness.

My ancestors—especially my father—had a rich understanding of the Truth. Maybe I inherited their beautiful understanding. Maybe this is why business and badwill make me so unhappy.

As I look back over 46 years of business war and see what it has won for me I wonder if Gandhi wasn't right. He taught that peace and happiness come only from poverty. No riches to guard. No thieves, bandits, kidnappers to fear. No worry, no hate, jealousy, greed or badwill to return and poison us.

And so it turns out that I have wasted the flower of my life chasing a wrong desire—fighting for money that buys only uneasiness, strain and unhappiness. This awakened me to wonder what I had really been fighting for all these years. Was it money? Or was I trying to find peace?

Then came the great awakening. I learned that I had not been fighting for money. I had been fighting for nearly half a century to find peace and didn't know it. And I saw for the first time that we can't buy peace with money. "Well," I said to myself, "if money won't buy peace, how can I get peace?" And the answer came, "I can only get peace by wiping out my bad-will thoughts"—the 34 poisons.

Then I asked myself, "How can I ever get rid of badwill thoughts?" And I decided that it is only a matter of being willing to and being willing to pray to our Lord for help. Whenever I get willing in my heart and pray to Him from the bottom of my heart I can do it.

"Without money and without price" we can get the victory over the beastly, badwill thoughts in ourselves. Then the golden door of heavenly thought opens into our heart and "the peace that passeth all understanding" steals through us. No one can take this peace away from us. It will be with us always. Its comfort never wanes but grows more tender and soothing and beautiful with the years. That is success!

Instead of spending a life-time in trying to build a money fortune or in trying to climb the ladder to a big job, we should spend it chiefly in trying to get the victory over the badwill (34 poisons) in our heart. Then we will find peace—the only success that life has to give.

"But," you are probably saying to yourself, "we've got to live in this world. We've got to have a job in order to get our supply of food and clothing. Suppose a man gets out of a job and has a family to support? He can't live on faith that Good-will thinking will drop manna from heaven!"

We could if we understood that our Lord Jesus (God) loves

us more than we love ourselves. We go through bodily motions to get food and clothing and what we need, but in reality our supply comes direct from our Lord Jesus (God).

These motions to supply our needs are due to our ignorance of the fact that we are a part of the machinery of the universe. As such, our supply comes to us as naturally and freely as air if we don't cut it off with badwill thinking.

For example: I know a doctor of thought who needed a home to live in and work in. She had no money. She had only faith and understanding that our Lord would give her this home if she wanted it for healing and teaching and helping others. She bought the home, and the money to pay for it came in the most unexpected ways. Supply comes if we understand that our Lord Jesus (God) works always for our good.

Moreover, here's something else that's hard to believe: This same doctor of thought often used to write checks to pay bills at the end of the month when she had no money in the bank. The money always came in before it was time to mail the checks out!

I have already told the story of George Mueller of Bristol, England—how he raised $7,500,000 for his orphan home and other religious work by prayer alone—how he never asked a single person for a donation. The Lord sent donors to him in answer to his prayers.

"All things work together for good to them that love the Lord"—to them that love to let Goodwill work through them instead of badwill.

I do not expect many beginners in the study of the power of thought to believe the above cases. Until they have seen the power of Goodwill work they can hardly be expected to believe such stories as this. But it will work for beginners, as well as for experienced students, if they are willing to let it work.

There is one sure way that a business or a person can make money; namely, learn that a business lives on what it GIVES and not on what it tries to get—so does every man. This rule succeeds because GIVING is a Goodwill thought. Trying to get with little or no giving is a badwill thought. It is a desire to cheat and steal and is therefore doomed to failure.

Few of the keenest business men and few holders of jobs understand this law of business. Most of us think only of getting—never of giving. Getting comes naturally as a reward for giving. "If we give more than we get we will soon get more than we give." It is the Law of *Come-Back* working in business.

Let me give you a case of how a 9 million dollar business was built from a deep desire to give: A salesman walked into the office of the Beechnut Packing Company at Canajoharie, N. Y., 40 years ago. He said, "I've been selling machinery to makers of chewing gum. I know how they make chewing gum. Why don't you go into the chewing gum business?"

Up to that moment Beechnut had never thought of making gum. Bartlett Arkell, president of the Beechnut Packing Company, said to the salesman, "Your idea sounds rather good. Go off and figure out what it will cost to make the finest chewing gum in the world."

"But," said the salesman, "that isn't the way to go into the chewing gum business. Nobody makes chewing gum that fine. They make a fair gum and advertise it." Mr. Arkell replied, "We don't make anything unless we can make it the finest of its kind in the world. If you don't want to make gum for us that way get out of here and stop wasting your time and mine."

The salesman came back in a few days and gave Mr. Arkell the cost of making the finest chewing gum in the world. Arkell built a gum factory in Canajoharie and started to make Beechnut Chewing Gum. One day the salesman walked into Arkell's office, shaking all over. He said, "I made a mistake in my figures. I can't make the finest chewing gum in the world at the price I gave you."

He expected to get fired. But instead Arkell put his hand on his shoulder and said, "That's the best thing you've said yet, for now I think you are really going to make that gum as good as we want it made. I never thought so before."

In 30 days after Beechnut Gum was put on sale in the stores Beechnut had to wire their 200 salesmen to stop selling it until they could arrange for another and larger factory. That was 40 years ago. The yearly sales of Beechnut Gum in 1939 were about 9 million dollars a year. They are much larger now in 1950.

Here we have an astonishing example of how a vast business was built on giving with getting as a secondary and unimportant thought. It was all very simple, for Mr. Arkell really didn't do anything but make the best gum on the market at that time. The total Beechnut sales of all the things they make is 20 million dollars a year—all from giving the finest foods they can make.

However, if it is so simple why doesn't everybody just give and gather in a harvest of money? They haven't the deep desire to give. They haven't the love of giving the world a great picture or a great score or a fine flavor just because of the "kick" that comes from giving.

They don't want to give anything at all. They just want to get. When Mr. Arkell gave Beechnut Bacon and Beechnut Chewing Gum to the commercial world I doubt if bacon or gum were much in his thought. He was on fire with a desire to give a wonderful flavor.

And let us take a look at Henry Ford. His whole life has been devoted to giving. The chief desire of his life was to give the finest car he could make at the lowest price so that millions might enjoy motoring. And what is more, Mr. Ford gives high wages to his workmen. He believes in high wages and low prices. That's giving. If every employer followed this plan there would be no hard times.

Mr. Ford said in the *American Magazine,* "Business is purely a service and not a bonanza. What I greatly hope for in children everywhere is a new attitude toward life, free from the gullibility which thinks we can get something for nothing, free from the greed which thinks any permanent good can come of overreaching others. . . ."

In this same issue of the *American Magazine* Mr. Ford was asked if he would consider running for President of the United States. He replied, "I can be much more useful tending strictly to my own business." Note the word USEFUL. He has no interest in anything in life except to be USEFUL.

A newspaper reporter said to Mr. Ford, "You have made a great fortune." Mr. Ford replied, "Yes, but I didn't start out to do that," meaning that he started out to give the finest car he could make at the lowest price with high wages for his workers. His fortune came as a secondary thing.

And what of the story of George F. Johnson, builder of the great Endicott-Johnson Shoe Company and its industrial democracy near Binghamton, New York?

This business was limping along toward failure when Mr. Johnson started to manage it. He brought into it the spirit of giving. He gave his customers the best shoes he knew how to make for the lowest price. He gave the highest wages he could pay. He gave his workers good homes which in some cases cost him more than he asked the workers to pay for them and they paid on easy payments.

He gave them cooperative stores where they could buy cheaply, a park, a golf course where the greens fee is 25¢, an athletic and skating field, a giant sanitary swimming pool, a restaurant where they can lunch or dine for 15¢, etc. He runs a hospital for them which has 22 surgeon specialists, 25 doctors, 152 nurses and 5 dentists. The hospital costs the company 1 million dollars a year.

He turned over his fine home to them as a library and went to live among them as their friend and neighbor in the same kind of house they live in. He put the management of the business under a board of directors made up of workers and all the workers share in the profits. Half of all the profits go to the workers. Each worker gets the same share of the profits.

What is the result of all this giving? Fourteen miles of factories, 19 thousand employees, no strikes, no shut-downs for seasons or hard times in 40 years, sales of 58 million dollars a year, the second largest sale of shoes in the United States, peace, plenty, happiness for 85,000 human beings and 85 years of glorious life for George F. Johnson!

Compare all this giving with the tight, greedy, getting policy of the New England shoe manufacturers. The shoe business of this country originated in New England and yet the old Yankee policy of getting has dried up the shoe busines of New England until today there are hardly enough shoes made in all of New England to keep one large factory busy.

One old factory in New England which has a large sale of shoes under a famous trademark buys its cheaper shoes from Endicott-Johnson. Why? Because Endicott-Johnson can sell the shoes to them at a lower price than this old Yankee factory of the getting policy can make them. A part of its great factories stands idle today.

A group of New York bankers offered George F. Johnson 45 million dollars for the Endicott-Johnson Shoe Company. He read their offer thoughtfully. Handing it back to them Mr. Johnson said, "No! There is not a human note in it."

A committee of the New York State Legislature asked Johnson why other manufacturers couldn't do what he was doing. Johnson replied, "Because they don't love the workers." And he might have added, "Because they want to get without giving."

Then there is the case of Milton S. Hershey, who made the finest bar of chocolate he knew how to make for 5 cents. He paid high wages and built a paradise for his workers at Hershey, Pa.

What is the result? Thirty-six years of marvelous prosperity and happy living for his employees and 82 years of joyous life for himself, and a 78 million dollar fortune which he has given to a wonderful school for orphans at Hershey!

All from the simple Goodwill thought of GIVING!

What a jolt to those of us who think business is a money-getting game! If we make ourselves really useful to employers or customers our pay will come. But most of us never think of making ourselves a thing of value. We only think of ways and means to get money. And few there be that get it that way.

The making of money by trickery, dishonesty, cruelty to labor and by getting the best of our brother brings the worst kind of sorrow, emptiness and unhappiness. People who make money this way seem to be happy but you cannot see the regret and sadness in their hearts. Even after they get the money it gives only hollow pleasure. We may get money without giving but it will not bring us peace, which is the only real success.

A friend of mine told me about the millionaires wintering at Miami, Florida. They were naturally seeking peace and pleasure. The only pleasures they could find were at the gambling house, the race track, the golf course, the bathing beach and in dancing, playing cards, giving dinners or fighting booze. Of course they found no peace in any of these amusements.

They did hire speakers to tell them something one night a week but I doubt if their thought, trained in the poison of badwill, could understand it or remember it. They with all their money can buy no peace. MONEY SUCCESS IS THE WORST FAILURE OF LIFE. Emerson called it "That bitch goddess—Success."

"Does my heart feel finer for the thing I have done?" Noble thought! It should be engraved in letters of gold on every heart and over the door of every business. The business or the man who follows that thought will always be happy and successful.

"We are rich only through what we give," says THE WISE MAN, and I might add, poor only through what we try to get.

"But," you probably say, "give us an example of how a poor fellow out of a job may succeed by this law of giving." Here it is: An oil burner company advertised for a salesman. They got 400 answers. Three hundred ninety-nine of them had no thought of anything but getting the money out of the job. Just one salesman thought of giving something and forgot about getting.

He knew nothing about selling oil burners, so he went out and learned all about them before he put in his bid for the job. He made a careful study of the company's oil burner. He called on homes which were using it. These home-owners set him on fire with the good points of the company's burner.

He called on homes which were using other burners and found out all the arguments against the other burners. He found a heating engineer and got the engineer to teach him the science of oil heating.

Then he sat down and wrote out his bid for the job. In it he told the company what he had done, what he had learned and how he would sell their burner. He told them a lot of things about selling their burner which they didn't know themselves. Of course he got the job and became their most successful salesman, earning big money.

This oil burner salesman thought only of giving. The other 399 thought only of getting. Business has no room for those who merely want to get. The getters are rolling stones who gather no moss. Whenever I find a man who has had a lot of jobs I always know he is a getter and not a giver.

Here is another example of how a poor girl won success by the law of giving. She had a consumptive husband, a child and her mother and father to support. She couldn't make enough money as a stenographer to take care of them and educate her child.

She got a job as a sales girl in a department store in Pittsburgh. They put her in the sportswear department. Customers came in to buy one dress. She sent them out with 2, 4, 6 and often a dozen dresses. In a few weeks they made her assistant buyer of the department. In a few weeks more her sales grew so big they made her buyer of the department.

The manager of the store whose salary was $85,000 a year took a deep interest in her and taught her the science of buying and running the department. Then the big department stores in New York began to bid for her services. When she retired and married a second time her salary at a New York department store was $12,500 a year.

After she retired the store she had left offered her $27,000 a year if she would come back. Other New York stores begged her to come with them at her own price. Yes, the law of giving never fails. Trying to get without giving is what fails.

If you are out of a job try giving and you will land a job and hold it even in hard times. No business that gives can fail—neither can any man. If a business or a man is not getting, the reason is simple—they are not giving enough even though they think they are.

A business must give such satisfying goods that customers can't do without them. Employees must give such valuable work that employers cannot do without it. Customers are always seeking such goods and employers are always looking for such workers. The much-quoted saying of Emerson is true, "If a man preach a better sermon, invent a better mouse-trap or build a better house than his neighbor, even though he live in a forest, the world will beat a pathway to his door."

That's another way of saying, "As we give, we receive—as we sow, we shall reap." If we give nothing we get nothing. If we give much we get much. The old Law of *Come-Back* works just as surely as dawn and dusk.

If our employer does not pay us what we think our work is worth we should make sure we are giving enough. If then he doesn't "come across" we should not ask for more money, for that will only make him mad. We should quietly look for another employer and resign.

Then our employer will offer everything. And even if we do not look for another employer, another employer will be looking for us, just as the New York department stores were looking for the Pittsburgh girl whose story I have told above. For employees who give are so few that they stand out from the mob of selfish getters, become known and are wanted.

Sometimes fair pay for giving good work may not come directly from those to whom we have given it. But it will come back through some other door—a door through which we least expect it to come. Valuable and unselfish service is never lost. The right pay for it is sure to come back. It is "bread cast upon the waters."

Another mistake in the hunt for success is to think that we have got to be a high-power, go-getter salesman of goods or of ourselves. I always thought I had to be a hell-raiser to succeed. But as I look back over 46 years of business fighting, the fighting and driving never got me a thing. My success seemed to come to me because I could give better service than anyone else in our line of work. I didn't sell a thing or sell myself. Prosperity just came to me in a simple, quiet way.

Of course I know now that it was supply from our Lord being handed to me. But I had to fight and tear myself to pieces for years to learn that my go-getter selling only made the buyers fight back against my selling drive and buy nothing of me.

Look at the most successful men in business! They were

nearly all mild-mannered men; namely, Henry Ford, George F. Johnson, Milton S. Hershey, J. P. Morgan, John D. Rockefeller, etc.

Business men who do not understand that "giving is what gets" are always worrying about competition (several companies trying to get the same business). Mr. Lipe, one of the founders of the Beechnut Packing Company, once said to me:

"We have no competition. We pay no attention to competition. We make the finest goods we know how to make and we can always sell fine merchandise." There is no competition for any person or business if they give to the limit. Their services or goods will always be wanted.

Besides, each of us has a fixed place and job in the universe like the stars. Nobody can take our place or do the special work that the Head of the Universe has laid out for us, just as no star can take the place and path of another star. If we cut out badwill we will find our place in life and succeed in spite of so-called competition, for competition cannot touch the job or business which has been set apart for us.

Example: Nobody can successfully copy Mr. Ford's way of making a car or his way of running his business. Nobody can successfully copy Mr. Rockefeller's way of carrying on his business and making money. Nobody can successfully copy Brisbane's style of writing or George Gershwin's style of composing music or Charles Schwab's salesmanship or Edison's inventive skill or the way mother used to make pie.

All of us, from the highest to the lowest, have been given some knack of doing something with which to earn our living, just as each of us has been given our own special face, figure and style of walking.

Perhaps it is a way of being a fine stenographer, or a way of handling figures, or a way of running a machine in a factory, or a way of selling goods in a department store, or a way of doing a chambermaid's work in a hotel. Nobody can take this gift away from us. Truly there is no competition if we find the gift that our Lord Jesus (God) gave us to earn a living with and then stick to it.

Our trouble is that we get full of badwill. We get full of "the will to fail" as Dorothea Brande says in her good book WAKE UP AND LIVE. We who fail are full of "the will to fail" and don't know it. We like to fail and be poor and mourn about it. If we get rid of the will to fail and other kinds of badwill, our Lord will show us our place in life and success will come peacefully, joyously.

The founder of a 30 million dollar business said, "There is only a hairline between failure and success." That hairline lies between badwill and Goodwill. On the one side is "the will to fail"—fear, worry, greed, hate, lying, stealing, cheating and all kinds of badwill. On the other is health, happiness, peace, love, joy and all our needs supplied.

The hardest thing in business is to choose the kind of work we can do the best. One author believes that the way to find our work in life is to follow our heart's desire. But our heart may tell us we desire some kind of easy work that seems to pay big money when in reality there is no such thing as big money for easy work.

Some of us can find our talent by getting rid of badwill and letting Goodwill thinking guide us. If we can't, I believe that some of us can find it by watching our inner urge to do a certain kind of work.

For example, if we have an inner urge to write, to draw, to sing, to dance, to figure, to teach, to type, to sell, to buy, to invest, to cook, to mother, to serve, to nurse, follow that urge. Katharine Cornell said she had an inner urge to act; Eleanor Powell was born to dance; the Wright Brothers to invent; Marshall Field to buy and sell.

Many colleges have departments called vocational guidance. These departments test you and try to tell you what kind of work you can do the best. They do not always hit it right but their findings may be helpful. The University of Cincinnati in Cincinnati, Ohio, and the Stevens Institute in Hoboken, N. J., have such a department.

There are also personnel firms which make a business of vocational guidance. They will give you psychological tests and try to find out what work you are best suited for. You can probably find their names in the Classified Telephone Directory.

Show me a man who has failed in life and I'll show you a man who has never found the kind of work he was cut out to do. Also you will find that he lives to get and not to give.

If I had my life to live over again I would try to overcome selfishness. I would try to give up all badwill thoughts. I would try to find out what my talent is. Having found it I would stick to the kind of work that would use my talent for life.

I would give everything I had to this work, no matter how little money I got out of it. For what good is money gained from work we don't like? To love our work brings peace. But to make money out of work we hate will ruin our life.

I would also stick to one job or one business if I knew it was the right job or business for my talent. For we can't possibly succeed if we change from job to job or business to business. Stay in one place. "Life is too short to learn more than one business well" and "a rolling stone gathers no moss."

I would also NOT try to make a fortune. I would take out an insurance policy in a good company which would take care of me in my old age and forget fame and fortune. They are no good. Or I'd work for a big company that pays pensions. This would relieve the worry about what will happen to us when we get old and would make it possible for us to enjoy our work and our daily life.

Last, if I were reliving my life I would keep 3 immortal thoughts always before me: "A business lives on what it gives and not on what it tries to get—so does every man." "Life is to give and not to take." And "Does my heart feel finer for the thing I have done?" This would fill me with peace and peace is the only success that life has to give.

CHAPTER 17

Worry

WORRY makes us suffer more than anything else in life. Worry is with us day and night, eating our hearts out. Nearly everyone asks me how to get rid of worry.

We worry most about our health, our family, our income and death. Let us take them up one by one.

What causes bad health? The badwill thoughts we send out. They are poison. They are 34 rank poisons. If we can stop sending them out and send out only thoughts of Goodwill, then the glowing health of Goodwill comes back and blesses us with the Goodwill harmony of health.

In case we get sick and can't cure ourselves by doctoring our thought, we should not worry about it. We should be thankful for the sickness, as I have said, because it is paying off some of our old debts to the Law of *Come-Back.*

If we won't stop thinking badwill thoughts and believe in the health-giving power of Goodwill thinking, there is nothing left for us to do except rely on the flesh for health. This stirs up the worst kind of worry, for we know in our heart that our fleshly body is so easily overcome by disease.

There is no way to get free from worry about our health except to pay off our debts to the Law of *Come-Back,* if we have to, and keep our mind always sending out Goodwill thoughts. There can be no bad health in a body full to overflowing with Goodwill. There is no record that Jesus was ever sick, as we have said. Sickness could not live in His pure thought. Neither can sickness live in OUR pure thought—free from the 34 poisons.

Many people worry for fear they will get the disease of insanity. As I have said before, it is better to be in the "coocoo house" full of the joy of thinking we are Napoleon without sense enough to worry than to live a life full of the hell of worry about insanity.

For example: Dale Carnegie says in his fine book HOW TO WIN FRIENDS AND INFLUENCE PEOPLE, "The head physician of one of our most important hospitals for the insane told me this story. He had a patient whose marriage proved to be a failure. She wanted love, children and social success but life ruined all her hopes.

"Her husband didn't love her. He refused even to eat with her and forced her to serve his meals in his room upstairs. She had no children, no social standing. She went insane; and in her imagination she divorced her husband and resumed her maiden name. She now believes she has married into the English aristocracy and she insists on being called Lady Smith.

"And as for children, she imagines now that she has a new child every night. Each time I call on her she says, 'Doctor, I had a baby last night.' Life once wrecked all her dream ships on the sharp rocks of reality but in the sunny, fantastic isles of insanity all her barkentines (ships) race into port with canvas billowing (blowing) and with winds singing through the masts.

"Tragic? Oh, I don't know. Her physician said to me: 'If I could stretch out my hand and restore her sanity I wouldn't do it. She's much happier as she is.'"

Most people think of insanity as an awful thing. They think that once insane, always insane. This is not true. Insanity is merely a sickness like any other sickness. About one-third of the insane are lastingly cured and over half of those who go into insane asylums are let out.

Furthermore, the public no longer frowns on those who have been insane. It merely regards them as having gotten over an illness. If we can get this understanding about insanity we will stop worrying about it. And if we stop our worry about it we will probably never go insane. Insanity, like all other sickness, is the poison of our badwill thoughts coming back to us.

The worry of parents about the family comes from a desire

to make their children follow the badwill of the parents. The parents want the children to hate those they hate. They want the children to envy something they envy, to love something they love, to criticize as they criticize, to be selfish as they are selfish, etc.

The children in most cases fight this high-handed rule of badwill which the parents think is right. Then the parents worry because the children won't follow their badwill which the parents believe to be right. Sometimes older brothers and sisters take it upon themselves to rule their younger kin in this way.

Of course children have to be looked after until they grow to a certain age but from then on parents have got to take their hands off and let the child's nature unfold. Parents only give children a fleshly body. The badwill and Goodwill nature of a child is all of his own choosing. In many cases his make-up is different from that of the parents.

We can't change a child's nature. We can't change a child's style of walking or the tone of his voice or his looks or the talent in his thought, etc. His nature must bloom like the rose and all of our worrying about it will not change it to bloom like the orchid.

Ben Franklin said, "Experience keeps a dear school but fools will learn in none other and scarce in that." We all learn only in the school of experience. Therefore why worry when children won't listen to our advice. We all need bitter experiences to teach us lessons and make us grow. Let the children have their fill of hard experience. It makes them strong. Besides, they will have it anyhow in spite of our advice and our worry.

The greatest men grow to greatness either without the advice of parents or in spite of it. Most great men just grew up untaught, unguided like a tough hickory tree. The greatest saps in the world were nursed up into saps by the badwill rule of their parents. "Hands off" the family will stop worry about the family.

Now as to the worry about income. This worry can be overcome easily if we are willing to follow the great truth that "A business lives on what it gives and not on what it tries to get—

so does every man." This is explained in the chapter on Success.

If we give enough we will always get a good income. But many of us feel that we are giving more service than we are paid for. We nearly all feel that we are underpaid, as I have said. However, if we are honest with ourselves we know we are not.

Our heart tells us that we are getting more than we are worth. That makes us worry about how long we can keep on getting too much for what we are giving. Then we worry about how soon we will lose our job or our customers.

On the other hand, when our heart tells us that we are giving more than we are getting, there can be no worry about income. The Law of *Come-Back* comes in here again. It is ever-present. It is a law of rigid justice.

Do you suppose Mr. Ford ever worried about income? No! Because he loved to give. Do you suppose that George F. Johnson of the Endicott-Johnson shoe business ever worried about income? Certainly not, for his heart told him every minute that he was giving everything in his power to help and comfort and love his workers.

Also his heart told him that he was giving his customers the finest shoes he could make with no thought of getting. Worry cannot live in a heart full of love and giving like that.

Mr. Ford said, "A man wrapped up in his work is protected from worry."

If we worry lest we may not be able to make a money fortune, we are worrying about something that will give us no end of worry should we make it. The badwill necessary to make a pile of money kills us at an early age and after all the years of badwill misery to make money, the wealthy find themselves sick, unhappy, bowed down with care or bored with life.

The wealthy really get little out of life except food, clothes and a place to live. We who are less lucky in money get those things without the worry and badwill which gnaw at the hearts of the rich. A darky said, "I got a hat on my head, shoes on my feet and plenty good clothes to wear. Why need I care?" That's the spirit that kills worry about income.

A very smart man said to me, "I had a million dollars. These hard times (1934) have wiped it all out except $100,000. But if I lose it all, my wife and I have enough brains to always make a living out of doing something."

That's true of all of us. Therefore why worry about income? We can always cut expenses to the bone and do something to earn food, clothing and a place to live. We can live on almost nothing if we have to and like it. There is always a way.

Worry is selfishness—love of self—love of self-comfort. We worry because we fear our self-comfort will be turned into hardship. Let's learn to think of the comfort of our brothers. Let's be useful to them and we will lose the worry that comes from greed for self-comfort.

If we lean on money to take care of us we are leaning on no safety at all. Giving, as I have said, is the only safe thing we can lean on in this world. It is divine. If we give, it will come back to us in supply "full measure shaken down and running over." There is no other safe thing on which we can depend for our daily needs. Thus giving alone wipes out worry about income.

A country doctor in Elizabeth, N. J., gave away most of his services all his life to those who suffered and couldn't pay. In his old age he was taken sick and had to stay in the hospital for 3 years. The mortgage on his home came due.

He had no money to pay either the hospital or his mortgage. But the citizens rose up in a mass and paid everything for him. This is a homely example of how giving comes back. The doctor invested in giving. When his need came this sure investment bore big interest. If he had collected all his bills for services through the years and invested the money in stocks, bonds and real estate he probably would have lost it all.

Insurance companies have learned that when a man has a policy that takes care of him in his old age he is likely to live longer. Freedom from worry about income makes us live longer. Giving will free us from worry about income far more than an insurance policy. Try it. You will be amazed.

Now as to death. Why worry about death? For the spiritual meaning of the word death is resurrection. In the chapter on *Death* I think we prove that death is resurrection.

We should not try to hold on to this life, for trying to hold
on to it and knowing that we can't fills us with fear and worry.
Our span of life is laid out for us here and we can do nothing
about it. Therefore why worry about it? Take what comes and
know that it is best for us. "Thy will be done."

Jesus told us to stop fussing about our life here when He said,
"He that findeth his life shall lose it; and he that loseth his life
for my sake shall find it." He meant for us not to love the world
and its life because we will lose it. But to love Him and the
spiritual life after death which we can't lose.

The silliest folly in life is to worry about dying, because we
can do absolutely nothing about it. Why take life so seriously?
Why not laugh through it?

I spent 50 years searching for the truth about death. What I
have written in the chapter on Death satisfies me and frees me
from the worry about death. If it does not free you, I am sorry,
for you may have to go on "dying a thousand deaths before the
real one," as Caesar said. And all because we are unwilling to
change from our childhood teaching to the understanding that
death is resurrection into spiritual life which never dies.

Here are some thoughts on worry that have helped me:

A wave of the sea goes down to come up. It never stays
down. Our life is just a lot of waves of good and bad experiences. We go down but we always come up again. Even death
is like a wave that goes down and comes up in the eternal spiritual life. If life had no ups and downs, the sameness of it
would be unbearable.

A woman on a train worried all the way from Atlanta to
New York for fear there would be snow in New York when she
reached there. But on arrival in New York there was no snow
at all. She had spoiled 34 hours of her life worrying about snow
in New York that wasn't there at all. Worries are nearly always
just notions like that. We build these notions up into what
seems to be something real. But nearly always the notions and
the worry are about nothing.

Mark Twain said, "I am an old man now and in my time
have worried over many things—but most of them never came
to pass."

When I begin to worry my wife calls it "hatching." After 53 years of living with me she can look at my face and see in my eyes that I am hunting up something to worry about. Then she asks, "What are you hatching now?" She is right. When I had nothing to worry about I used to hatch up something.

As fast as one worry ends in nothing, we who worry start right in to dig up another worry. As fast as we get rid of one ailment we find another one to worry about. As fast as we wipe out worry about one kind of unhappiness we hunt up another kind to stew about. As fast as one kind of business worry fades away we stir up another kind to fret about.

Worry is a habit which we worriers enjoy, just the same as we enjoy the habit of smoking or drinking coffee. We don't know that we enjoy it but we do. We can stop worry whenever we lose our pleasure in it and decide that we want to "give it the gate." We can stop doing anything we really want to stop. WE CAN CHANGE. WE DON'T HAVE TO BE THAT WAY. We can build up the habit of NOT worrying just the same as we built up the habit of worrying.

I had a crack in the corner of my mouth for 30 years. I had heard that such cracks might lead to cancer. I was scared to ask a doctor to look at it for fear he would tell me it was a cancer. For 30 years I worried about that crack and pictured all sorts of operations which would make my face look horrible and bring certain death.

Finally after 30 years of awful worry I got courage enough to ask my osteopathic physician about it. He said it was no cancer and that 4 out of every 10 people had such cracks. He treated it for a month with caustic soda. It healed up beautifully and never came back.

Thirty years of poisonous worry about nothing! I never carry any load of worry like that now. If I get to stewing about some ailment and can't free myself by doctoring my thought I go to the doctor right away and get him to wipe it out of my thinking. We should never carry any burden of worry. We should get rid of it some way and as quickly as possible.

Here is a story from the New York *Times* which proves what worry does to our fleshy body: "The Portugal newspaper *Se-

culo reports that Alvaro Esteva, a Spanish manufacturer with insurgent sympathies, played dead in a Malaga Cemetery for 2 whole months. Mr. Esteva hid in an empty coffin in the family tomb to escape government troopers.*** He emerged when the insurgents took the town.*** His hair, jet black 2 months ago, turned a snowy white."

Cases of hair turning gray from worry are quite common. If worry grays the hair, which is an organ of the body, is it not reasonable to believe that worry brings age and disease to other organs of the body?

I had a brother who used to say, "I don't care what happened yesterday or what is going to happen tomorrow. I live only for today—to get all the fun I can out of today." He did not make a lot of money but always had a plentiful supply for daily needs and lived nearly 70 happy years.

I try to take life as he did, hour by hour and day by day. I try not to worry about things past or things to come. I try not to stew and plan how tomorrow is going to work out. If I don't know how to straighten out some problem I try not to stew about it. I just don't do anything about it. I let it work itself out. I "muddle through" it as the English do. I try to let the power of Goodwill thinking guide my every thought and act.

The bliss that comes from letting the power of Goodwill thinking work for us this way is astonishing. Doors will open everywhere. Healing, happiness and daily needs (but not wealth) will walk through them and lay their blessings at our feet. For the smooth-flowing harmony of the universe works always for us and through us, just as it does for the stars, if we keep badwill poison out of the way.

I know a very healthy, happy and successful Englishman in London. I asked him how he always kept himself so calm. He said, "I do the best I can. If that doesn't make me healthy and successful I can't help it. So why should I worry and fill myself full of the poison of worry?" What simple yet marvelous wisdom! If we worriers would try it we would find blessed freedom from the slavery and hell of worry and we would find everything working out for our good although it may not seem for our good at the time.

In November 1936 Mrs. Franklin D. Roosevelt said that this is her husband's daily rule: "Each day must be lived. You must accept what comes. Do what you think is right or best. Decide what should be done and stop worrying."

Without this non-worrying rule President Roosevelt could never have mastered the dark, gigantic, never-ending troubles of the panic years of 1932-40 and World War II. They would have buried him in failure and illness. But note how cheerful and carefree he breezed through it all—this man who suffered from having had infantile paralysis. We of sound body and peewee cares should be ashamed of ourselves when we worry.

If we can't stop worry any other way we should say to ourselves, "Let the worst come. I don't care," and really mean it. Really be willing to get sick, go insane, fail or even die, as I have said before. That will break the whirling of the worry thought and give the harmony of the universe a chance to work through us and bring us back to peace and happiness.

But you may say, "I am not willing to let the worst come. I am not willing to get sick, go insane, fail or die. Therefore how can I say I am willing to?" Our very unwillingness to give in to them is what makes us worry. When we get willing to let them happen our worry will fade away like fog before the sun. And the question is, wouldn't it be better to be sick, insane, busted or dead than to suffer the hell of worry all our life?

Another helpful thought when we are badly worried is to say to ourselves, "Is worrying about this thing going to do any good? Is worry going to clear up this mess? No! All the worry in the world is not going to change it one quarter of an inch. Then why worry about it?" We should say, "I'll drop the worry and give the power of Goodwill a chance to clean it up. If I get my worry out of the way the trouble will straighten itself out."

We who worry are yellow. We are cowards. We are afraid of sickness, unhappiness and failure. We haven't got the guts to walk right up to them and meet them face to face and defeat them.

Worry burns up our strength and power to think. Worry wastes mountains of power in each one of us every day. If this power were used for doing better work, for giving and for

Goodwill thinking it would flood us with health, joy and unbelievable success.

Medical journals, medical books and doctors agree that worry upsets metabolism. Metabolism is the part of our digestion which changes our food into blood, as I have said. You can easily see what happens to us when our food does not change into healthy, red blood.

We also read in medical journals and medical books how strife, strain, fear and worry shrink the size of our small blood vessels and thus cause high blood pressure. Of course we all know that high blood pressure leads to death unless it can be stopped.

I asked a doctor to give me a list of the diseases which fear and worry can bring upon us directly or indirectly. Here is a list of a few of them:

    angina pectoris (heart trouble)
    nervous breakdown
    neurasthenia (tired nerves)
    gout
    certain heart diseases
    neuritis (pain in nerves)
    certain diseases of the brain
    nervous indigestion or dyspepsia
    anemia (pale blood)
    mucous colitis (rawness in the bowels)
    gastric or peptic ulcer in the stomach
    insomnia (sleepless nights)
    tuberculosis

But we should not get scared stiff that we are going to get these diseases because we have worried all our life. If we haven't any of them now we may never get them if we stop worrying. If we have any of them we can relieve them by stopping our worry. All I am trying to do is to show you that worry is poison.

Worry IS rank poison, more to be feared than any poisonous drug. Our body may be able to throw it off for years but sooner or later the poison of worry will come back and poison us if we keep on worrying.

I know that the poison of worry played a big part in causing every sickness that ever came upon me. I know that I got erysipelas, gout and my worst illness 45 years ago from worry. Why flirt with this deadly poison of worry?

Riding the hobby of worry is dangerous business. We are often more liable to get sick from worry than from coming in touch with consumption or smallpox.

Worry is lack of experience with the power of Goodwill thinking. Those who worry have never seen the power of Goodwill thinking keep sickness, misery and want away. If they had had this experience it would have wiped worry out of their thought forever. Instead of worrying they would be leaning wholly on the power of Goodwill thought which holds a power far beyond our understanding.

The New Testament was originally written and spoken in the Aramaic language. There is no word in Aramaic that means what we mean in English by worry. The Assyrians who used that language left everything in the hands of Our Lord Jesus (God). Therefore they had no worries such as Americans and Europeans have and no word for worry.

When one gets sick in Assyria (Jesus' country) neither the patient nor the doctor worries nor does the doctor hurry to the sick person. The doctors are all doctors of thought and not doctors of the flesh, and the patients who all know the power of thought expect only their thought to be doctored. Both know that the sickness is only wrong thinking. They take sickness so lightly that often the doctor does not answer the patient's call for 3 or 4 days and the patient doesn't care.

This is why Jesus did not go to see Lazarus for 4 days. Even though Jesus knew that Lazarus was dead or dying and even though Jesus was only about 20 miles away from him, He let 4 days pass before He went to him.

That's the kind of freedom from worry we should all get. We could all get it if we were willing to lean on the power of Goodwill thinking as the Assyrians and Galileans did. We who worry have no faith in the power of Goodwill thinking or in

Our Lord Jesus or in anything. Therefore we can rely on nothing but worry.

Whatever happens is for our good. It may not seem so when it happens. But later on we will always see that it IS for our good, as we have said. If we look back on the things that have happened to us through life we can prove to ourselves that this teaching is true.

Henry Ford said many times that he never worried because he believed that whatever happened was for the best.

Dale Carnegie wrote a second book entitled HOW TO STOP WORRY AND START LIVING. In that splendid book he gives a golden thought on worry. It should kick worry all out of us worriers. He says, "When trouble comes we can always stand it, so why worry?" We all know this is true. We can all "take it" and get out of it some way when it hits us. How foolish to give it even a passing thought!

The unseen Holy Spirit of our Lord Jesus in our heart guides and governs us through all hard experiences. Hence there is no use worrying about what happens to us. We should bow to our Lord's will and give thanks. We should know that whatever happens is for our good. Even though our small thinking may not see that it is for our good at the time it happens.

But after all, we will never get free from worry until we get free from badwill—the 34 poisons. We are afraid of the badwill thoughts we are sending out although we don't know we are. Our heart, however, feels the poison which is coming back from them and this uncertain feeling in our heart fills us with worry.

If we are free from ALL the 34 badwill poisons nothing can happen to us but good. For with the 34 badwill poisons gone out of us nothing but good from heaven flows into us.

Thus if we can get free from ALL badwill we can be free from ALL worry. Let me repeat that—we will never get free from worry until we are free from the 34 poisons of badwill and therefore at peace with our Lord Jesus (God).

CHAPTER 18

Sleep

WE WHO have trouble going to sleep are suffering at night from the badwill thoughts that stormed through us during the day. We key up our thinking all day long with fighting, badwill thoughts such as hate, anger, irritation, fear, worry, hurry, strife, strain, selfishness, greed, etc.

Then we lie down in bed at night with the silly notion that these keyed-up, badwill thoughts will suddenly unwind and let us down into blissful sleep. Our mind gets so excited with badwill poisons during the day that it can't quiet down and sleep at night. Badwill thoughts during the day change the natural, loose harmony of our thinking into a disease of tightness.

This tight, high-strung thinking won't "loose us and let us go" to sleep at the day's end just because we want it to. It just keeps on whirling round and round in our thought like the blades of an aeroplane.

Both medical science and the Simmons Bed Company have tried to find a *fleshly* cure. But a *fleshly* cure will never be found. The cause must be wiped out and the cause is tight, strained, excited, badwill thinking in the daytime.

One way to get relief from sleepless nights is to change our days of badwill to days of Goodwill thoughts—to days of peaceful thinking. Then the peaceful thoughts of our days will carry over into the night and let us down into loose, refreshing sleep.

However, here are some suggestions that may help us to sleep until we learn to live and work more peacefully in the daytime:

The study of sleep by the Simmons Company said, "The fear that we won't sleep when it comes time to go to bed seems to be the cause of insomnia (sleepless nights)." This is true. A few wakeful nights fill us with the fear that we can't sleep and of course the more this fear gets hold of us, the more we lie awake. For "the thing I greatly feared came upon me."

How can we break up this fear? By understanding that lying awake at night is a habit we've gotten our mind into. If we can get our mind into this habit we can get our mind out of it. If we can build up the habit we can break it down.

Just know that we can change. Repeat our war cry I CAN CHANGE and believe it. Nothing in life is fixed. THE ONLY SURE THING IN OUR LIFE IS CHANGE. If we would stop fretting about the sleepless nights and not care whether we sleep or don't sleep, the fear of sleepless nights would go away and we would sleep.

Jerome W. Ephraim in his good book TAKE CARE OF YOURSELF says that the average grown-up person probably feels best after 8 hours' sleep daily but this is not a law of nature. He says that many get along quite well on less and the supposed harm of losing sleep is often greatly exaggerated. Actually, very few hours of sleep are needed to keep us alive— the rest are luxury.

Furthermore, he says that unless we have pain we cannot stay awake to the point of real danger. Rest in bed does nearly as much as sleep itself and 6 hours of rest plus 2 hours of slumber will keep us going.

He says that Darwin, Franklin, Napoleon, Frederick the Great, Horace and Virgil are among the famous poor sleepers of history and it does not seem to have hurt their thinking or their health—several lived to a ripe age.

The worst notion we can get in our head is the notion that we must get 8 or 9 hours' sleep or we won't feel good next day. That makes us strive and strain to go to sleep and get this amount of rest. This striving and straining to get this set number of hours in sleep is a sure way to keep awake. We should follow Mr. Ephraim's advice that 2 hours' sleep and 6 hours' rest are enough.

Edison and Hitler only slept 4 hours. The monks in Tibet only sleep 3 hours. They taught this to Theos Bernard who learned to sleep only 3 hours a day. Therefore why fear that we won't get 8 or 9 hours' sleep when it really doesn't matter whether we get a long sleep or a short sleep?

My cook, as I have said, is a deeply religious colored woman. She says, "I go to sleep as soon as I touch the bed and sleep right through the night because I have perfect peace in my thoughts."

Perfect peace in our thoughts! How many of us have that? None of us poor sleepers have it. That's why we don't sleep. We go to bed with our thinking full of fear, worry, care and tight thoughts from our badwill days. No one can sleep with such bad, boiling thoughts.

We should stop trying to fight our mind to sleep when we go to bed or wake up in the night. For when we try to force our body to sleep we force our body wider and wider awake. We should just lie on our back in bed with arms and legs spread out and say to ourself, "I don't care whether I sleep or not. I am willing to lie awake all night. I am willing to lie in this nice, comfortable bed and just rest. For the rest I am getting will make me feel almost as fit tomorrow as a good night's sleep."

This willingness to lie awake wipes out the worry about our not sleeping. It takes off the strain of trying to force our body to sleep. We are already under the strain from our day of strife or we would not be awake. Therefore to try and fight our body to sleep only adds to our strain and keys us up all the more. It makes us more and more awake. "The way to sleep is to stop trying to sleep."

Many a night I have gone to bed strung up from working "in high" all day, as I have said. I have lain down, closed my eyes and talked silently to myself, using these thoughts "I am willing to let loose. I am willing to stop all strife and strain. I am willing to let go, let down and let Goodwill thoughts flow through me.

"I am willing to let loose on my whole spinal cord and nerves from the back of my head all the way down to my heels. I am willing to let loose on my whole nervous system all the way down to my heels. I am willing to let loose all over all the way down to my heels." I got so well trained in this loosening work that bubbles seemed to be running down my spinal cord.

I would go on thus with the doctoring of my thought: "I am willing to feel like I am floating on air. I am willing to lie awake. I am willing to enjoy my rest in this nice room and bed. I am so thankful for this nice room and bed and the rest they give me, even though I don't sleep. But I can change. I don't have to be this way. I don't have to have sleepless nights."

After doctoring my thought in this way I would awaken later to find that I had been lost in satisfying sleep for hours. What let me down into sweet sleep without my knowing it? The loosening of my thoughts instead of tightening them up by trying to force my body to sleep. Also being willing to lie awake if I couldn't sleep.

Another way I let myself down into deep sleep is to lie quietly on the pillow with eyes closed and think of all the things I am thankful for. Before I get half way through naming the things I am thankful for (silently) I fall asleep. This is a wonderful way of getting to sleep because the giving of thanks brings peace and quiet and shuts out the whirling, straining thoughts rushing in from our day's work.

Furthermore, it stops us from lying there and wondering if we are going to go to sleep and if so, when. That "wondering when" is a strain that keeps us awake. We should not try to know just the moment when we are going to fade into sleep for we never know that moment. And lying there trying to figure it out keeps us awake.

Sometimes I recite poetry to myself silently until I become sleepy enough to sleep. The best poem I know is SERENE I FOLD MY HANDS AND WAIT by John Burroughs. It is very soothing and quieting.

Another way I loosen up and fall asleep is to imagine I am lying on my back on the shore of a peaceful lake. I picture myself looking up at the moon. I am listening to the whispering of the breeze in the forest. I hear the swish of the water lapping softly on the beach.

Or I call up the memory of a golden sunset or a beautiful scene or some of the happiest moments of my life. I call up some experience like this that lulled me into a restful feeling of peace at some time in my life. I feast on these soothing pictures instead of thinking of the day's round of harsh, irritating thoughts.

Or I try to get into the soft, loose mood of a cat asleep before the fireplace with the logs burning lazily. Did you ever feel the front paws of a cat when he is sleepy? They are the most loose and lazy things in the world. Just thinking about the loose, lazy feeling of a sleepy cat's paws makes me loose and sleepy. Try it.

Or I fill myself with a deep feeling of love for everybody and everything. That melts the raging thoughts of badwill as nothing else can.

Here is another way that I overcome a whirl of tight thinking on one thing and fall asleep: I lie in a comfortable position with eyes closed and think softly to myself over and over again, "I'm oh so sleepy. I'm so beautifully loose all over." While thinking these soothing thoughts I open my fingers and toes wide apart. I usually find them clinched tight without my knowing it.

Another splendid way I get to sleep is to repeat silently to myself, "Be still and know that I am God." In other words, I am saying to my raring, boiling badwill, "Be still and let the meek, loving, dove-like will of our Lord Jesus ('God) work." If we can feel the true meaning of this beautiful thought it will loosen us into sleep quickly and surprisingly.

For it quiets the beastly, fighting badwill which is storming in our thought and keeping us awake. It sets aside our pushing, battling, raving badwill and lets the calm, gentle, peaceful Goodwill of the Holy Spirit come in and take hold of us. When that tender Goodwill takes hold of us we loosen up, let go and fade away into the paradise of sleep.

Many is the time that I have gotten in the habit of waking up at 6 o'clock in the morning with the feeling that I could not possibly go to sleep again. I would slip a black bandage over my eyes to keep out the light. I would turn over, keeping my eyes closed, for if we let the light into our eyes it gets us awake.

Then I would let my spinal cord, nerves, muscles, etc., loose from the back of my head down to my heels. The first thing I knew I would awaken to find it was 7 or 8 or 9 o'clock. I wouldn't believe I had fallen asleep for 1 or 2 or 3 hours. In fact, it took me months to believe that I had really been asleep during these several hours. I couldn't believe it was sleep. I thought I had just lain there with my eyes closed.

The black bandage mentioned above is a handy, comfortable, light-weight covering for the eyes. It fits the eyes like a domino masquerade mask. You can get it in department stores. I slip it on at dawn or when I am in a hotel room where there is a glare of light. It is a marvelous help in making one sleep in spite of a strong light shining on us. Besides, it rests the eyes and makes them feel strong.

If we get in the habit of waking up at night or in the early morning and can't go back to sleep, we can fall asleep again by using the same methods given above for going to sleep when we first go to bed.

Another scheme to bring on sleep is to lie in bed and try to keep our eyes open. We will find this a hard thing to do. It makes some folks sleepy. A doctor told me that when he can't sleep he gets up and takes 4 or more deep breaths before the open window. He said this always makes him sleepy.

If these methods won't make us sleepy, sit up in bed and read something. Don't read fiction or anything that is thrilling for that wakes us up. Read something that is heavy or hard to read. Heavy reading makes us sleepy. I always keep something heavy to read beside my bed so I won't have to get up and stir myself into more wakefulness.

This heavy reading stops our thoughts from whirling. It gets our thinking on some other subject than the one which is whirling in our thought. As soon as this whirling of thought is broken up we are very liable to relax into sleep. We all know that reading makes most of us sleepy. This is why.

Also when we go to bed we should have no timepiece in the room. Watching the clock all night to see how many hours we have slept and how soon dawn is coming keeps us keyed up in thought. Go to bed to get loose from thinking. Cast off the world and all of its cares and worries and time. Make no rule as to how many hours we must sleep. Sleep whatever number of hours we can and be thankful for them.

The number of hours' sleep we need differs with different people. Some need more, some need less. It isn't the number of hours' sleep we get that rests us. The soundness of our sleep is what makes us feel rested and all made over.

In the book TAKE CARE OF YOURSELF we read that we should have a soothing bedroom finished in blue or blue-green —the colors that make us drowsy. Shut out noise and light as far as possible. A pitch-dark room where light can't come, even in the morning, helps us to sleep. Cover up or turn to the wall all bright things such as mirrors.

We should get the air in our room just right, for plenty of fresh air helps to bring on sleep. The room should be neither too hot nor too cold. A cool room is better than a warm room for sleep. But in winter we can get too much cold air if we have nose or throat trouble. We should lock our bedroom door if we fear burglars so as to get that fear out of our thought, for we can't sleep if any thought is upsetting our peace.

We should fix things so we are not afraid of fire. We should not have too much or too little covering—just the right warmth from light-weight covers. Being too hot or too cold or weighted down with heavy covers will keep us awake. Besides, heavy covers are tiring. TAKE CARE OF YOURSELF says, "Have a regular hour for going to bed. Do not wait till you get tired; the aim is drowsiness, not tiredness." It says that if we have a regular time for going to sleep we will get sleepy at that time every night like clockwork, whether we are tired or not.

This same good book says, "It has been shown that if you blindfold the average person, put cotton in his ears and ask him to lie down on a soft couch for thirty minutes, he will almost always fall asleep." We might try that.

Furthermore, we should buy the best springs and mattress we can afford. The very best are not awfully expensive, and since one-third of our life is spent in bed, the best mattress and springs are none too good. The best mattress is made out of small spiral springs and hair. Each spring is wound with canvas. The best springs are box springs.

The president of one of the finest hotels told me to buy a Simmons Beautyrest hair mattress and Simmons La Grande box springs. We should be sure to get the Beautyrest mattress made out of *hair* with a La Grande box springs. They are certainly full of heavenly comfort. They soothe and woo the body to let loose and let down into peaceful rest and sleep.

Other companies make these same fine mattresses and springs. If we have never slept on them we have no idea how these beds coax the body to relax into deep, blissful sleep. Nor do we realize the difference in our rested-out feeling in the morning. If one does not wish to pay the price of a *hair* mattress and box springs he can get cheaper ones that are very good.

Also the right kind of a pillow is almost as needful as a fine mattress and springs. For if we can't get our head comfortable we can't relax into sleep. I find two Simmons pillows filled with 65% goose feathers and 35% goose down are a wonderful aid to sleep and rest. Some people cannot sleep on 2 pillows, however. And some sleep better on no pillow. Many doctors believe we should sleep without any pillows. Each one of us has to decide on his own pillow comfort.

Sleep and rest are so vital to our health, happiness and success that no reasonable amount of money is too much to pay for a soft, soothing bed and pillows. We can buy them on easy payments just as we buy our car and they are far more important in our lives than a car.

I found that I should not build up a notion that I am not going to sleep tonight. For many is the night that I have gone to bed sure that I wouldn't be able to sleep, only to wake up next morning and find that I had slept beautifully. If we don't sleep one night that is no reason why we won't sleep well the next night.

The loss of one or two nights' sleep is good for us because it generally brings a second or third night of deep, glorious sleep.

We should stop all thought about business when we leave

our place of business. This is vital, for if we take our business home and talk it all through dinner and all evening we wind up our thinking to high C so it can't run down.

Make the dinner hour and the evening joyous with good humor and jokes and peaceful thinking. To go to bed in a merry, laughing mood has a wonderful way of making us let loose and relax into sleep.

We should learn to love our bed and love to go to bed. A man whose business was in a bad way found that he had to cut his salary and stop all luxuries. He said, "I am willing to cut out everything except the joy of reading and relaxing in bed before I go to sleep."

Another thing that helps me to sleep and feel better is to take a good walk after the evening meal and while walking I take deep breaths. I draw the air in through my nose, keeping the mouth closed. I suck up my guts as they say in the army, through my nose and blow it out through my mouth. Keep your stomach flat while breathing both in and out. Walk and breathe until you feel fresh, loose and tired.

Breath is the stream of life. Life begins and ends with breath. An expert on breathing said, "I believe that if everyone knew how to breathe correctly there would be no disease upon the earth."

If the heavy meal could be taken at noon and a light supper at night I believe most people would sleep more soundly. Children are fed this way and have no boiling, badwill days. They know nothing from the time they fall asleep till dawn. Maybe we who have trouble with sleeping might find this plan of eating the way to sound sleep. But some people can't sleep on an empty stomach. Some sleep better by taking a snack before bed time.

Try slow breathing to help you go to sleep. This is not deep breathing. It is merely slow breathing. Sit up in bed, close your eyes and say silently, "I am going to get my thinking very quiet and think very slowly." Then I breathe slowly for 5 minutes. See if you don't fall sound asleep!

This slowing down of thought and slow breathing also helps us to fall asleep in the night if we awake and can't get back to sleep. It lowers the amount of blood in the brain and that makes us drowsy.

Here is a way of bringing on a loose feeling all over which will make us sleep. It is thousands of years old. The way it lets one loose is astonishing. Lie flat on a hard floor on the back with arms spread out like the crossbar of a cross and legs spread out V-shape. Loosen up and let go all over. Close the eyes. Breathe slowly and think softly, "My mind is in utter darkness. My body is floating on air." Keep repeating this slowly and breathing slowly. It is claimed that 15 minutes of this treatment is more restful than hours of sleep in bed. I have tried this treatment many times. When I get back in bed I relax into beautiful sleep.

Don't try it in bed. The softness of the bed keeps one from letting loose. Giving your whole weight to the floor takes away the tightness of muscles and soothes the nerves. But in winter the floor is too cold for this treatment. It might give us a cold.

Too much exercise keys us up so we can't sleep. On the other hand, lack of exercise and fresh air in our lungs may keep us awake because we are not tired enough to sleep.

A bank president was under heavy strain and overwork. He was strung up to the sky. Couldn't sleep and couldn't leave his business to take a vacation. His doctor told him to go home every afternoon at four o'clock. The doctor told him to go to bed, read, have his dinner served in bed and stay in bed till morning. The doctor also told him to stay in bed over each entire weekend.

What this did to loosen up the banker and let him down into sleep and rest was wonderful! Try it. It may show you that you are over-tired from strife, strain, noise and overwork and don't know it. This may be keeping you awake.

As I have said, I got into the habit of having dreams at night which were full of strife and strain. I was chasing trains and ships which I could never catch or the cops were after me, etc. These dreams were merely echoes of the strife and strain of my badwill days still storming in my thought at night.

For example, I took a mild dislike to a man one day. Four

nights afterward I dreamed of a fierce fight with him that upset my night's sleep. One day I got mad because I had to read two small articles. That night I went through a hard strain in my sleep in which I was trying to read something to a valuable customer but couldn't. The slightest badwill thought during the day may come back at night or several nights afterward and fill a night's sleep full of strain and keep us awake.

Drinking hot milk, plain or with chocolate, or just hot water before going to bed is an old recipe for bringing on sleep. It draws the blood from the brain down into the stomach. When the brain loses a lot of blood it doesn't think much and when it slows down on its thinking it goes to sleep.

Frederick S. Bigelow had a good article in the *Cosmopolitan* Magazine entitled IF YOU CAN'T SLEEP IT'S YOUR OWN FAULT. He says that every medical man knows what can be done in the way of bringing on sleep by the right sort of bath. That the more unpleasant your bath, the more it will probably bring on sleep. That you must deny yourself the sharp, bracing shock of the cold bath followed by a hard rubdown. A cup of epsom salts added to the bath will soothe and relax the body.

He says you must not use water of comfortable warmth. Your tub or shower must be so lukewarm that you come out of it almost shivering. You must pat yourself dry as your nurse did for you when you were a babe in arms. After this you will find yourself a little damp and chilly.

Next you make a beeline for bed and put your light out, thoroughly hating yourself. Soon the chilliness begins to go away and a mild, pleasant warmth takes its place. As you become more and more comfortable sleep begins to take hold of you. There is a blissful period of 15 or 20 or 30 minutes during which, if you put the brakes on your racing thoughts, you have a very good chance of dropping off to sleep.

This bath was used by Dr. John Harvey Kellogg of the Battle Creek Sanitarium. He says he taught it to insane asylums. He said it made high-strung, insane patients let go and sleep when all dope had failed. But a bath keeps SOME of us awake and a hot bath makes some people sleep.

Another way to do the same thing, says Stanton Tiernan in *Nation's Business*, is to "throw off your bed coverings, cool off to the shivering point, then pull the blankets over you again. Sleep will come with the warming up." But in doing this one must be careful not to take cold.

Frederick S. Bigelow also says in Hearst's *International Cosmopolitan*, "Many of those who suffer from sleeplessness will agree that it is the bad habit of night thinking that keeps them awake. What can we do to break this habit?"

He tells us to imagine that each thought which comes to us while we are trying to fall sleep is writing itself on a slate or blackboard. Imagine, he says, that we are wiping it off with a wet sponge as fast as it comes on the slate or blackboard. He says that he himself has tried his little scheme and it certainly does wipe every thought out of our thinking in bed as fast as it shows up. This works fine with me.

Another way of doing this same thing is to imagine we are looking at a black spot. If we drive all thoughts out of our thinking and hold our thought on this black spot it will stop our thinking. Then as soon as our storming thoughts stop we will fall asleep.

I believe, as Mr. Bigelow seems to, that one big reason why we don't sleep may be told in just 3 words: THINKING IN BED. If we didn't think in bed about the boiling thoughts of the day or didn't think at all in bed we would sleep. We can do it by practice. A good plan is to keep saying to ourselves, "Slam the door on all night thinking. Go to sleep." This works.

A fine osteopathic doctor said to me, "When you go to bed go there with the idea that you are going there to sleep and not to think."

Dr. Jackson and Dr. Lewis in their good book OUTWITTING YOUR NERVES say that "sleep is a state of vanished interest," meaning that we have lost all interest in everything. That's it. We should lose all interest in everything when we start to go to sleep. Then we won't think in bed and will fall asleep.

The Rotarian prints an article under the heading PAGE DR.

MUSIC by Doron K. Antrim, editor of *Metronome*. Here is part of what he says on sleep:

"If your trouble is insomnia (sleeplessness), music is your specific antidote (cure). One doctor carried a small music box about the hospital with him. It only played one tune—Spring Song—but he claims that playing it 3 times will lull any willing patient to sleep, provided, of course, that he is not suffering acute pain. In one hospital where a twilight musical was tried for 3 months the use of sleep-inducing sedatives (quieting medicine) fell off a third. Nocturnes, lullabys and serenades replaced them."

He says a Brooklyn doctor recommends Chopin's waltzes to bring sleep and a friend of his had a continuous-playing phonograph put in his bedroom to cure his insomnia. At first he needed 9 pieces to get to sleep. Now he needs only 4.

I was always afraid of the night. That didn't help me to sleep. But one day I read some word pictures of the night in CHILDREN OF SWAMP AND WOOD. They changed my dread of the night into a love for its poetic beauty.

If fear of the night hinders our sleep, we should read this beautiful book. After reading it I think we will feel beauty, poetry and peace all about us at night.

I wrote the above in 1940. Now, ten years later, I have learned that sleepless nights may be caused by evil spirits who delight to torment us. So before going to bed I pray as follows:

"Our Father, dear Lord Jesus, who art in heaven and who art in the heart of all my brothers who, like me, are suffering from sleepless nights: I pray Thee, if it be Thy will, to bring Thy perfect life into the minds and hearts of all my brothers (including myself) who are being kept awake by evil spirits.

"I pray Thee, dear Lord Jesus, if it be Thy will, to command the evil spirits to come out of us and enter no more into us tonight and forever. I thank Thee, dear Lord Jesus, that Thou hast heard me for I know that this is being done. Amen." If we can have faith in this prayer we may sleep beautifully.

But we must not fear evil spirits. For our Lord protects each one of us with two guardian angels. Each one of us has two angels following us day and night to hinder evil spirits from doing us harm. The divine Light from one frail angel will cause a thousand evil spirits to flee back into hell in terror.

Evil spirits can only make us lie awake and feel uncomfortable when we let ourselves down into badwill thoughts. For that sinks us down into their thought. Even then our guardian angels hinder them. Our job is to think only Goodwill thoughts. These good thoughts surround us with the divine Light and Love of Our Lord shining through our guardian angels. Surrounded by this Light and Love, only good can come to us.

We should try all these ways of bringing on sleep and stick to the one that helps us; or when one fails, try another. I have no set way. Sometimes I use one, sometimes another.

But if all these suggestions fail and we get up in the morning after a wakeful night, we have got to learn to take it sweetly and be thankful that we are no worse off than we are. We should also know that our sleeplessness may be the "thorn in our flesh" that is driving us to wipe badwill out of our thought and let Goodwill thinking give us health, happiness and prosperity.

After a sleepless night we should get up in the morning singing and turn some lively music on the radio while we dress and forget our sleepless night. We should not build a mountain of misery out of it. For hardly anybody sleeps well every night, just as hardly anybody feels good every day. There are nights when a whole neighborhood sleeps poorly because there is more badwill thought in the air than usual.

My osteopathic doctor says "I have never slept well in all my life. But I don't pay any attention to it." His advice to poor sleepers is to forget it. For he says "they probably don't need the sleep."

And remember that we who have trouble with sleeping often sleep more than we think we do. We are so sure we can't sleep that we won't believe we have slept even when we have.

Stephen Leacock in TOO MUCH COLLEGE tells of two men who had to sleep in the same bed one night. Next morning one said to the other, "Did you get much sleep?" "Not a damn minute." "Neither did I," said the other; "I could hear every sound all night." Then they noticed that during the night the ceiling had fallen on them, covering the bed with plaster!

We who sleep well are not sense-less when asleep. We are half awake and half asleep. Therefore we who think we can't sleep are very apt to recall that we were half awake during the night and regard it as poor sleep. We are so anxious to sleep that we are not satisfied with our sleep unless we sleep like a man knocked senseless. Nobody sleeps that soundly.

"Dr. Donald A. Laird, of Colgate University, has spent 10 years gathering data on how people sleep—how long and how well," says the *Eagle Magazine*. Dr. Laird's telltale machine which records how people sleep shows that "the best sleeper moves 4 to 5 times an hour." The *Eagle Magazine* adds, "Don't ever boast of sleeping like a log. This machine will make a liar out of you."

We often feel better the next day after a wakeful night than we do after 10 hours' sleep. Some of my most successful business days have followed nights when I slept hardly at all.

I remember once I had a date with a bank president. I lay awake the whole night before the meeting in mortal dread, thinking of the fight I expected to have with him next day. This filled me with fear and worry as to how I could ever face that meeting.

I got up next morning tired, weary and sunk. But I went to the president's office and made one of the best selling talks of my life. When I got into the talk I forgot my weariness and dived into my talk with all the freshness of one who had slept well. I've done the same thing hundreds of times.

This shows how we can change our weariness by changing our thinking. Who knows but what we will wake up some morning in these days of scientific discoveries and find that sleep is only a needless habit. If the monks in Tibet need only 3 hours' sleep maybe that's all we need.

People between 60 and 70 years of age often do not need more than 4 or 5 hours' sleep. Loss of sleep is not without its benefits. For example:

Dr. Carrel, in his MAN THE UNKNOWN, says that fixed,

regular habits cause certain parts of the body to lose their power and thus weaken our strength. Therefore, he says, an upset in our habits and our sleep brings these little-used parts of the body into action and thus makes the body stronger and more healthy.

One husky old gentleman told me that he always arose at the same time in the morning no matter what time he went to bed. Sleep meant nothing to him. But we sleepless people make sleep a hobby. We make an awful "settin' hen" fuss about it and the more we fume, the less we sleep.

The fact is, we like to stew about sleep. It's an enjoyable pastime with some of us. Whenever we really want to stop this stewing we can and when we do we will probably sleep without further trouble.

If we of the wakeful nights could know that sleep is a part of the beautiful harmony of life and let it alone, we might be surprised to find how easily this harmony would work. The soundest sleepers, like the old gentleman mentioned above, never think anything about it. They just let nature take care of their sleep just as it takes care of the silent and regular motion of the stars.

Whatever we do we should not take dope, near-dope or any kind of medicine to make us sleep if we can possibly help it. For all medicines that make us sleep are harmful if we keep taking them. Some of them weaken the tiny, white beads in our blood called white corpuscles. These white policemen of the blood were put there to fight off disease.

Besides, if we take much of these sleep medicines they lose their power to make us sleep. Then we are without anything to bring on sleep when we might need it in a case of sickness. Again, the taking of sleep medicines can lead to the dope habit which is one of the most awful things that can happen to a human being.

Four doctors told me to take 2 five grain aspirin tablets to make me sleep. One of them told me I could repeat the dose in two hours if necessary. He said also that 3 hours' sleep from aspirin is more restful than 6 hours' sleep from dope. But don't follow this advice without asking your doctor.

The muscles of those who can't sleep are all tightened up by their tight thinking. A good osteopath or chiropractor can do wonders in relaxing our tight muscles. This relaxation generally gives me a beautiful sleep.

These suggestions are made to help ease the misery of sleepless nights. But few of us who are troubled with wakeful nights will ever get peaceful sleep until we stop our high-strung days of badwill thinking.

We should neither get overjoyed nor sunk at what happens in our daily work. We should go along through all the ups and downs of the day with our thought always calm, moderate and peaceful. Such gentle, kindly days of Goodwill thinking toward our work and toward everything and everybody should carry over into the night and give us blissful sleep.

CHAPTER 19

Without Love We Are Nothing

THERE are two kinds of love, (1) love of self and the bad things in the world, (2) love of our Lord Jesus (God) and the good in our brothers. The one is love of the 34 poisons from hell. The other two are Divine Love from heaven.

Love of self and the world full of 34 poisons is the cause of all sickness, unhappiness, fear, worry, war and hard luck. Perfect love for our Lord and our brothers would free each of us from all these miseries and bring heaven on earth. For love of our Lord and our brothers is a white fire that burns up all the 34 poisons. They cannot live in a heart, mind and body full of Divine Love.

You don't believe it? Well, consider the angels in heaven. They are just men and women like you and me. But they have purified themselves of the 34 poisons. That's why they are angels. That's why they are never sick or unhappy. That's why they never suffer from fear, worry, war and hard luck. That too is why they never grow over 30 years old and look so beautiful. Their perfect love for our Lord and our brothers is what makes heaven.

Jesus told us plainly that Divine Love is the crown jewel of life when He said: "Love the Lord thy God with all thy heart and all thy mind and all thy soul. This is the first great commandment. The second is like unto it. Love thy neighbor as thyself. On these two commandments hang all the law and the prophets." Meaning that a life of health, happiness and freedom from fear, worry, war and hard luck can come *only* from obeying these two great commandments.

Maybe you ask: "How can I love God?" We should start by

loving the good in our brothers. Loving our brothers is loving God, for the life in our brother is God. But maybe you say "It's hard for me to love my brothers. They are so rotten." However, the bad we see in them is generally in us. We see our own faults in them. Besides, our Lord only expects us to love the good in them.

If we don't want to love our brother, that's a sure sign we don't want to love God. "For if ye love not your brother whom ye have seen, how can ye love God whom ye have not seen." We should begin to love God by loving our brother. Then love Jesus (God) as a man. Love His gentle, humble, innocent, child heart.

Yes, love Him as your Father, for He is your heavenly Father. He is the Divine Being of God shown to us in the flesh. God had Himself born into the fleshly body of Jesus so we would have a fleshly man like ourselves to love and pray to. For the Divine Being of God is too big, boundless and brilliant for us to understand. Our puny minds cannot work with his vast intelligence or reach Him.

When I first started to try and love my brothers, it was tough going. But gradually as I began to love them I felt streams of joy flowing into my heart. A tremendous load seemed to lift off of me. Then as I also began to love Jesus too, the whole of my life and the world began to change.

All man-made things in the world began to look like a mountain of junk. The streets and haunts of New York which I had loved for 40 years turned ugly, dirty, gloomy. I began to see my "precious" self as a giant hog full of self-love. Then I began to pray to our Lord to help me overcome my love of self and the world full of the 34 poisons.

I am far from gaining perfect love. I will have to battle with the 34 poisons way into my next life before I get the victory over them. All of us will have to. This work is called regeneration.

Sickness comes from the 34 badwill poisons. If our heart and thought are full of Divine Love sickness could not live in them. Therefore we could not get sick, for there would be nothing to make us sick.

A heart and thought full of Divine Love can never be unhappy, for love thinks never of selfishness but only of another's good. That kind of a heart and that kind of thinking can never be unhappy. For the Goodwill coming back from those whom we love fills us with joy.

And how can fear live in a heart and thought full of Divine Love, for have we not seen how "perfect love casteth out fear"? We are never afraid if we have done what Love tells us to do.

Moreover, could there be any war if the war-mongers loved the boys they send to the slaughter?

Again, could there be any want, strikes or hard times if we all loved each other as ourselves? For example: We all know the story of Golden Rule Nash of Cincinnati. He had a small factory making men's clothing. His business was losing money. He had decided to close it up as soon as possible and become a farmer.

Even though his business was losing money he bought out a clothing "sweat shop" to help a friend who was about to fail. In this "sweat shop" there was a woman 80 years old sewing on buttons at $4 a week. Also a hunchback running a machine at $4 a week. All the workers in that "sweat shop" were getting starvation wages.

The angelic mother of Nash had taught him the Golden Rule; namely, "Therefore all things whatsoever ye would that men should do to you, do ye even so to them." Nash had a deep love for this rule and also for his workers. When he saw that poor old woman and the hunchback toiling for only $4 a week he could not bear it.

He raised the pay of each of them to $12 a week which was three times what they were getting. He then gave all the workers three times what they were getting. But what was more important, he loved his workers as himself. Their comfort, welfare and happiness were always his first thought. Personal gain meant nothing to Nash. He became their friend and brother—not their boss.

After raising their wages he gave little attention to the business. For he expected to close it up and take up the life of a farmer. One day another friend's company was about to fail. In keeping with the Golden Rule, Nash wanted to help this friend. So he went to his bookkeeper to find out if he had enough money on hand to aid his friend.

To his astonishment he found his company had an amazing amount of cash in the bank. After the factory closed that day he went to the forewoman and asked her what was bringing in all these profits.

She said it was his love coming back to bless him. "Why," she said, "that poor 80-year-old woman's eyes fairly flash with a new interest in life as she turns out more work then she ever thought she could. The same is true of the hunchback and every other worker in your factory."

What was the outcome of Mr. Nash's love for his workers? The Nash business grew from sales of $132,190 in 1918 to sales of $12,284,119 in 1925; from 29 workers to over 3,000; from a petty business to the largest company of its kind in the country. All in 8 years and all because of a simple, human feeling called love!

Of course you are wondering what happened to the sales after 1925. I asked a friend about that who knew Nash and used to lecture for him in Cincinnati. He said that Nash died and with him died the Golden Rule and his love for the workers. Naturally the spirit and great growth of the business died down.

Samuel Z. Batten says, "Will the Golden Rule work? Millions of people have answered that it will work in a prayer meeting or a missionary society. But if it will not work in a clothing factory or a store it is not a Golden Rule and has no value. Mr. Nash has proven that it not only works but it is the only thing that really does work."

Nash says that manufacturers tell him how they tried the Golden Rule and all they got out of it was strikes and fights. Nash says they missed the big point of it all; namely, "They didn't love the workers." George F. Johnson of Endicott-Johnson Shoe Company used these same words when telling the New York Legislature why other manufacturers could not do what he was doing with the Endicott-Johnson Shoe Company.

Nash said, "Stop using men and women to make money and begin using money in order to make men and women."

Mr. Nash ends his book by saying, "'Therefore, all things whatsoever ye would that men should do to you, do ye even so to them, for this is the law and the prophets.' In that and that alone lies the hope of mankind. The world has tried every scheme that the ingenuity of man could invent and has failed miserably. It has been demonstrated in our organization that the philosophy of Jesus will work and in every place that it has been made real it has worked just as it has done in ours. It is the only way out."

Love IS the only way out of all the woe in the world today. If all nations loved each other we would need no armies, navies, military planes, atom bombs, or wasteful preparations for war.

If the Germans, Russians, French, English, Japanese and Americans had loved each other we would have had no World War I or World War II. Think of the billions in money and millions of boys that we would have saved!

If all nations loved each other today we would need no United Nations and no black war clouds would be gathering again.

If manufacturers loved their workers there would be no strikes and no need for labor unions. If labor unions loved the manufacturers, strikes would be unknown. If we all loved each other as we love ourselves nobody would be out of work because we would find work for our brothers in need.

For example: In 1939 there were 10 million people out of work. At that time there were nearly 2½ million employers in the United States.

If each of these employers had hired an average of 4 workers whom they didn't need, this act of love would have given jobs to all the 10 million unemployed. It would have wiped out the relief rolls, and brought sunshine into some 40 million souls living in misery.

But oh no! We can't love our brother enough to employ 4 men whom we don't need. We must use mass production and labor-saving machines and efficiency experts to make more money to satisfy our greed. But in doing so we throw 10 million workers out of work and thus force ourselves to pay out billions in taxes to support them on relief! What is worse, this selfishness drove 10 million of our unfortunate brothers and their families into the sorrow and despair of taking dole!

If we all loved each other as we love ourselves we would see every nation on the earth ruled by love and what a beautiful blessing that would be to mankind!

Akbar was king of one of the many small kingdoms of India. He conquered all the other kingdoms in India and put them together in a great empire which he ruled with love from Our Lord until his death.

No king of all the kingdoms he conquered was ever thrown into prison or driven from his homeland. On the contrary, Akbar kept each conquered king on that king's own throne. He loved them all and they loved him and all the people loved him.

Akbar had a deep passion for religion and an unquenchable thirst for the Truth. This came down to him from saintly ancestors. This saintly inheritance made him dig deep into every religion and philosophy. He loved everybody and everything so tenderly that he would not allow the hunting of wild animals.

But don't think Akbar was a weakling. He had one of the most marvelous, fleshly bodies ever known. He could ride horseback for 100 miles without tiring. He could not have conquered the whole of India if he had not been a mighty general of arms.

Once when he and some friends were walking in the jungle a female tiger and two cubs suddenly came into their path. A mother tiger with cubs is the most dangerous thing alive. Akbar's friends fled and would probably have met death. But Akbar attacked and killed the tiger with a knife. Yet this Hercules ruled his vast empire with love throughout his life and the Law of *Come-Back* brought back love and peace and prosperity to all.

People often say to me, "Look at this or that awful thing that

is happening in our country. Hate and badwill have the upper
hand. The devil seems to rule. Is there no God?"

My answer is that hate and badwill never have the upper
hand. They only *seem* to for a little while and then the clouds
melt away and the sunshine of good comes out.

Hate *always* fails. But "love never faileth." Hate and evil
always destroy themselves. If this were not true, hate and evil
would wipe out the human race.

There is everything to be gained by love of our Lord and
our brothers—everything to be lost by love of self and the
world full of 34 poisons. It may be a long, long time before
"the wolf shall dwell with the lamb." The world may have to
suffer bitterly and kill nearly everybody and everything on this
beautiful earth before man will become willing to love the
Lord and his neighbor as himself.

But you and I can learn that love of the 34 badwill poisons
brings us only sickness, unhappiness, fear, worry, hard luck.
And we can learn that love of our Lord and our brothers will
bring us health, happiness, freedom and plenty.

As I have said before, there can be no healing unless our
heart is full of Divine Love. We can repeat all the correct healing thoughts and words in the world but they will heal nothing
unless they come out of a heart on fire with love for our Lord
and our brothers.

The heavenly Truth about love was written by Emanuel
Swedenborg, the Lord's servant. He said that love of self and
the world is poison from hell. Whereas love of our Lord Jesus
(God) and the good in our brothers is glory from heaven. See
the chapter on Sin.

Religion is of the heart and not of the head.

Here are a few immortal thoughts on love from the Bible that
always fill my heart with a deep sense of love.

"Ye have heard that it hath been said, Thou shalt love thy
neighbour and hate thine enemy, But I say unto you, Love
your enemies, bless them that curse you, do good to them that
hate you and pray for them which despitefully use you and
persecute you. For if ye love them which love you, what reward have ye? Do not even the publicans the same?"

"Love ye your enemies and do good, and lend, hoping for nothing again; and your reward shall be great."

"This is my commandment, That ye love one another, as I have loved you. Greater love hath no man than this, that a man lay down his life for his friends."

"For this is the message that ye heard from the beginning, that we should love one another."

"He that loveth not knoweth not God; for God is love. *** Beloved, if God so loved us, we ought also to love one another.*** If we love one another, God dwelleth in us, and his love is perfected in us.*** God is love; and he that dwelleth in love dwelleth in God, and God in him."

"For I am persuaded that neither death, nor life, nor angels, nor principalities, nor powers, nor things present, nor things to come,

"Nor height, nor depth, nor any other creature, shall be able to separate us from the love of God."

"Love not the world, neither the things that are in the world. If any man love the world, the love of the Father is not in him."

"Behold what manner of love the Father hath bestowed upon us that we should be called the sons of God."

"Beloved, let us love one another; for love is of God; and every one that loveth is born of God, and knoweth God. He that loveth not knoweth not God; for God is love."

"If we love one another, God dwelleth in us and his love is perfected in us."

"Now the works of the flesh are manifest, which are these; Adultery, fornication, uncleanness, lasciviousness,

"Idolatry, witchcraft, hatred, variance, emulations, wrath, strife, seditions, heresies,

"Envyings, murders, drunkenness, revelings, and such like; of the which I tell you before, as I have also told you in time past, that they which do such things shall not inherit the kingdom of God." What a picture of badwill (the 34 poisons)!

"But the fruit of the Spirit is love, joy, peace, long-suffering, gentleness, goodness, faith,

"Meekness, temperance: against such there is no law." What a picture of Goodwill (Divine Love)!

How can any of us see any good or gain in anything but love of our Lord and our brothers? The "old lifer" in prison pictured it so beautifully to Starr Daily. He said to Daily in their prison cell, "Son, there is nothing but love."

Jacob Boehme was a poor German shoemaker. He talked with God. He said "The Love of our Lord Jesus is the most precious treasure of the people of God, which no life can ever express, nor any voice give utterance to, for this fire of love of the Lord Jesus is brighter than the sun, sweeter than all besides. More supporting than all food and drink. And more to be desired than all the joys of the world.

"He who finds this love is richer than any king on earth, nobler than any conqueror, and stronger than any power."

And how heavenly are these words from the authoress of THE GOLDEN FOUNTAIN: She was baptized three times in a blaze of Light and Love from heaven. She said, "Every other love on earth is but a poor pale counterfeit of Love—a wan Ophelia wandering with a garland of sad perished flowers to crown the dust. I desire with all the force of my heart and soul and mind and body to love Him (our Lord Jesus). Oh, if I could be the warmest, tenderest lover that ever Thou didst have! Teach me to be Thy burning lover. This is my perpetual prayer."

As a fitting climax to this volume, I beg of you to read the following three brilliant masterpieces which you will find on the following pages:

"The Greatest Thing in the World," by Henry Drummond
"The Practice of the Presence of God," by Brother Lawrence
"As a Man Thinketh," by James Allen

These works have awakened the hearts of millions all over the world. They contain mountains of Divine Love and Wisdom.

Three Masterpieces of Great Thinking

The Greatest Thing in the World

By Henry Drummond

THOUGH I speak with the tongues of men and of angels, and have not Love, I am become as sounding brass, or a tinkling cymbal. And though I have the gift of prophecy, and understand all mysteries, and all knowledge; and though I have all faith, so that I could remove mountains, and have not Love, I am nothing. And though I bestow all my goods to feed the poor, and though I give my body to be burned, and have not Love, it profiteth me nothing.

> *Love suffereth long, and is kind;*
> *Love envieth not;*
> *Love vaunteth not itself, is not puffed up,*
> *Doth not behave itself unseemly,*
> *Seeketh not her own,*
> *Is not easily provoked,*
> *Thinketh no evil;*
> *Rejoiceth not in iniquity, but rejoiceth in the truth;*
> *Beareth all things, believeth all things, hopeth all*
> *things, endureth all things.*

Love never faileth: but whether there be prophecies, they shall fail; whether there be tongues, they shall cease; whether there be knowledge, it shall vanish away. For we know in part, and we prophesy in part. But when that which is perfect is come, then that which is in part shall be done away. When I was a child, I spake as a child, I understood as a child, I

Please bear in mind that wherever Mr. Drummond uses the word love he means Divine Love—Love of our Lord Jesus (God) and the good in our brothers.

thought as a child: but when I became a man, I put away childish things. For now we see through a glass, darkly; but then face to face: now I know in part; but then shall I know even as also I am known. And now abideth faith, hope, Love, these three; but the greatest of these is Love.—1 Cor. xiii.

Every one has asked himself the great question of antiquity as of the modern world: What is the *summum bonum*—the supreme good? You have life before you. Once only you can live it. What is the noblest object of desire, the supreme gift to covet?

We have been accustomed to be told that the greatest thing in the religious world is Faith. That great word has been the keynote for centuries of the popular religion; and we have easily learned to look upon it as the greatest thing in the world. Well, we are wrong. If we have been told that, we may miss the mark. I have taken you in the foregoing chapter from Corinthians, to Christianity at its source; and there we have seen, "The greatest of these is love." It is not an oversight. Paul was speaking of faith just a moment before. He says, "If I have all faith, so that I can remove mountains, and have not love; I am nothing." So far from forgetting he deliberately contrasts them, "Now abideth Faith, Hope, Love," and without a moment's hesitation the decision falls, "The greatest of these is Love."

And it is not prejudice. A man is apt to recommend to others his own strong point.

Love was not Paul's strong point. The observing student can detect a beautiful tenderness growing and ripening all through his character as Paul gets old; but the hand that wrote "The greatest of these is love," when we meet it first, is stained with blood.

Nor is this letter to the Corinthians peculiar in singling out love as the *summum bonum*. The masterpieces of Christianity are agreed about it. Peter says, "Above all things have fervent love among yourselves." *Above all things.* And John goes farther, "God is love." And you remember the profound remark which Paul makes elsewhere, "Love is the fulfilling of the law." Did you ever think what he meant by that? In those days men were working their passage to Heaven by keeping the Ten Commandments, and the hundred and ten other commandments which they had manufactured out of them. Christ said, I will show you a more simple way. If you do one thing, you will do these hundred and ten things, without ever thinking about them. If you love, you will unconsciously fulfil the whole law. And you can readily see for yourselves how that must be so. Take any of the commandments. "Thou shalt have no other gods before Me." If a man love God, you will not require to tell him that. Love is the fulfilling of that law. "Take not His name in vain." Would he ever dream of taking His name in vain if he loved Him? "Remember the Sabbath day to keep it holy." Would he not be too glad to have one day in seven to dedicate more exclusively to the object of his affection? Love would fulfil all these laws regarding God. And so, if he loved Man you would never think of telling him to honor his father and mother. He could not do anything else. It would be preposterous to tell him not to kill. You could only insult him if you suggested that he should not steal—how could he steal from those he loved? It would be superfluous to beg him not to bear false witness against his neighbor. If he loved him it would be the last thing he would do.

And you would never dream of urging him not to covet what his neighbors had. He would rather they possessed it than himself. In this way "Love is the fulfilling of the law." It is the rule for fulfilling all rules, the new commandment for keeping all the old commandments, Christ's one secret of the Christian life.

Now Paul had learned that; and in this noble eulogy he has given us the most wonderful and original account extant of the *summum bonum*. We may divide it into three parts. In the beginning of the short chapter, we have Love *contrasted;* in the heart of it, we have Love *analyzed;* toward the end, we have Love *defended* as the supreme gift.

The Contrast

PAUL begins by contrasting Love with other things that men in those days thought much of. I shall not attempt to go over those things in detail. Their inferiority is already obvious.

He contrasts it with eloquence. And what a noble gift it is, the power of playing upon the souls and wills of men, and rousing them to lofty purposes and holy deeds. Paul says, "If I speak with the tongues of men and of angels, and have not love, I am become as sounding brass, or a tinkling cymbal." And we all know why. We have all felt the brazenness of words without emotion, the hollowness, the unaccountable unpersuasiveness, of eloquence behind which lies no Love.

He contrasts it with prophecy. He contrasts it with mysteries. He contrasts it with faith. He contrasts it with charity. Why is Love greater than faith? Because the end is greater than the means. And why is it greater than charity? Because the whole is greater than the part. Love is greater than faith, because the end is greater than the means. What is the use of having faith? It is to connect the soul with God. And what is the object of connecting man with God? That he may become like God. But God is Love. Hence Faith, the means, is in order to Love, the end. Love, therefore, obviously is greater than faith. It is greater than charity, again, because the whole is greater than a part. Charity is only a little bit of Love, one of the innumerable avenues of Love, and there may even be, and there is, a great deal of charity without Love. It is a very easy thing to toss a copper to a beggar on the street; it is generally an easier thing than not to do it. Yet Love is just as often in the withholding. We purchase relief from the sympathetic feelings roused by the spectacle of misery, at the copper's cost. It is too cheap—too cheap for us, and often too dear for the beggar. If we really loved him we would either do more for him, or less.

162

Then Paul contrasts it with sacrifice and martyrdom. And I beg the little band of would-be missionaries—and I have the honor to call some of you by this name for the first time—to remember that though you give your bodies to be burned, and have not Love, it profits nothing—nothing! You can take nothing greater to the heathen world than the impress and the reflection of the Love of God upon your own character. That is the universal language. It will take you years to speak in Chinese, or in the dialects of India. From the day you land, that language of Love, understood by all, will be pouring forth its unconscious eloquence. It is the man who is the missionary, it is not his words. His character is his mesage. In the heart of Africa, among the great Lakes, I have come across black men and women who remembered the only white man they ever saw before—David Livingstone; and as you cross his footsteps in that dark continent, men's faces light up as they speak of the kind Doctor who passed there years ago. They could not understand him; but they felt the Love that beat in his heart. Take into your new sphere of labor, where you also mean to lay down your life, that simple charm, and your lifework must succeed. You can take nothing greater, you need take nothing less. It is not worth while going if you take anything less. You may take every accomplishment; you may be braced for every sacrifice; but if you give your body to be burned, and have not Love, it will profit you and the cause of Christ *nothing*.

The Analysis

AFTER contrasting Love with these things, Paul, in three verses, very short, gives us an amazing analysis of what this supreme thing is. I ask you to look at it. It is a compound thing, he tells us. It is like light. As you have seen a man of science take a beam of light and pass it through a crystal prism, as you have seen it come out on the other side of the prism broken up into its component colors—red, and blue, and yellow, and violet, and orange, and all the colors of the rainbow —so Paul passes this thing, Love, through the magnificent prism of his inspired intellect, and it comes out on the other side broken up into its elements. And in these few words we have what one might call the Spectrum of Love, the analysis of Love. Will you observe what its elements are? Will you notice that they have common names; that they are virtues which we hear about every day; that they are things which can be practiced by every man in every place in life; and how, by a multitude of small things and ordinary virtues, the supreme thing, the *summum bonum,* is made up.

The Spectrum of Love has nine ingredients:

Patience .... "Love suffereth long."
Kindness .... "And is kind."
Generosity ...... "Love envieth not."
Humility .... "Love vaunteth not itself, is not puffed up."
Courtesy .... "Doth not behave itself unseemingly."
Unselfishness .... "Seeketh not her own."
Good Temper .... "Is not easily provoked."
Guilelessness ..... "Thinketh no evil."
Sincerity .... "Rejoiceth not in iniquity, but rejoiceth in the truth."

Patience; kindness; generosity; humility; courtesy; unselfishness; good temper; guilelessness; sincerity—these make up the supreme gift, the stature of the perfect man. You will observe that all are in relation to men, in relation to life, in relation to the known to-day and the near to-morrow, and not to the unknown eternity. We hear much of love to God; Christ spoke much of love to man. We make a great deal of peace with heaven; Christ made much of peace on earth. Religion is not a strange or added thing, but the inspiration of the secular life, the breathing of an eternal spirit through this temporal world. The supreme thing, in short, is not a thing at all, but the giving of a further finish to the multitudinous words and acts which make up the sum of every common day.

There is no time to do more than make a passing note upon each of these ingredients. Love is *Patience*. This is the normal attitude of Love; Love passive, Love waiting to begin; not in a hurry; calm; ready to do its work when the summons comes, but meantime wearing the ornament of a meek and quiet spirit. Love suffers long; beareth all things; believeth all things; hopeth all things. For love understands, and therefore waits.

Kindness. Love active. Have you ever noticed how much of Christ's life was spent in doing kind things—in *merely* doing kind things? Run over it with that in view, and you will find that He spent a great proportion of His time simply in making people happy, in doing good turns to people. There is only one thing greater than happiness in the world, and that is holiness; and it is not in our keeping; but what God *has* put in our power is the happiness of those about us, and that is largely to be secured by our being kind to them.

'The greatest thing," says some one, "a man can do for his Heavenly Father is to be kind to some of His other children." I wonder why it is that we are not all kinder than we are? How much the world needs it. How easily it is done. How instantaneously it acts. How infallibly it is remembered. How superabundantly it pays itself back—for there is no debtor in the world so honorable, so superbly honorable, as Love. "Love never faileth." Love is success, Love is happiness, Love is life. "Love I say," with Browning, "is energy of Life."

"For life, with all it yields of joy or woe
And hope and fear,
Is just our chance o' the prize of learning love,—
How love might be, hath been indeed, and is."

Where Love is, God is. He that dwelleth in Love dwelleth
in God. God is Love. Therefore *love*. Without distinction,
without calculation, without procrastination, love. Lavish it
upon the poor, where it is very easy; especially upon the rich,
who often need it most; most of all upon our equals, where it is
very difficult, and for whom perhaps we each do least of all.
There is a difference between *trying to please* and *giving
pleasure*. Give pleasure. Lose no chance of giving pleasure.
For that is the ceaseless and anonymous triumph of a truly loving spirit. "I shall pass through this world but once. Any good
thing therefore that I can do, or any kindness that I can show
to any human being, let me do it now. Let me not defer it or
neglect it, for I shall not pass this way again."

Generosity. "Love envieth not." This is love in competition
with others. Whenever you attempt a good work you will find
other men doing the same kind of work, and probably doing
it better. Envy them not. Envy is a feeling of ill-will to those
who are in the same line as ourselves, a spirit of covetousness
and detraction. How little Christian work even is a protection
against un-Christian feeling. That most despicable of all the
unworthy moods which cloud a Christian's soul assuredly waits
for us on the threshold of every work, unless we are fortified
with this grace of magnanimity. Only one thing truly need the
Christian envy, the large, rich, generous soul which "envieth
not."

And then, after having learned all that, you have to learn
this further thing, *Humility*—to put a seal upon your lips and
forget what you have done. After you have been kind, after
Love has stolen forth into the world and done its beautiful
work, go back into the shade again and say nothing about it.
Love hides even from itself. Love waives even self-satisfaction.
"Love vaunteth not itself, is not puffed up."

The fifth ingredient is a somewhat strange one to find in this *summum bonum: Courtesy.* This is Love in society, Love in relation to etiquette. "Love doth not behave itself unseemly." Politeness has been defined as love in trifles. Courtesy is said to be love in little things. And the one secret of politeness is to love. Love *cannot* behave itself unseemly. You can put the most untutored persons into the highest society, and if they have a reservoir of Love in their heart, they will not behave themselves unseemly. They simply cannot do it. Carlyle said of Robert Burns that there was no truer gentleman in Europe than the ploughman-poet. It was because he loved everything —the mouse, and the daisy, and all the things, great and small, that God had made. So with this simple passport he could mingle with society, and enter courts and palaces from his little cottage on the banks of the Ayr. You know the meaning of the word "gentleman." It means a gentle man—a man who does things gently with love. And that is the whole art and mystery of it. The gentle man cannot in the nature of things do an ungentle, and ungentlemanly thing. The ungentle soul, the inconsiderate, unsympathetic nature cannot do anything else. "Love doth not behave itself unseemly."

Unselfishness. "Love seeketh not her own." Observe: Seeketh not even that which is her own. In Britain the Englishman is devoted, and rightly, to his rights. But there come times when a man may exercise even the higher right of giving up his rights. Yet Paul does not summon us to give up our rights. Love strikes much deeper. It would have us not seek them at all, ignore them, eliminate the personal element altogether from our calculations. It is not hard to give up our rights. They are often external. The difficult thing is to give up ourselves. The more difficult thing still is not to seek things for ourselves at all. After we have sought them, bought them, won them, deserved them, we have taken the cream off them for ourselves already. Little cross then to give them up. But not to seek them, to look every man not on his own things, but on the things of others— *id opus est.* "Seekest thou great things for thyself?" said the prophet; "*seek them not.*" Why? Because there is no greatness in *things.* Things cannot be great. The only greatness is unselfish love. Even self-denial in itself is nothing, is almost a mistake. Only a great purpose or a mightier love can justify the waste. It is more difficult, I have said, not to seek our own at all, than, having sought it, to give it up. I must take that back. It is only true of a partly selfish heart. Nothing is a hardship to Love, and nothing is hard. I believe that Christ's "yoke" is easy. Christ's "yoke" is just His way of taking life. And I believe it is an easier way than any other. I believe it is a happier way than any other. The most obvious lesson in Christ's teaching is that there is no happiness in having and getting anything, but only in giving. I repeat, *there is no happiness in having or in getting, but only in giving.* And half the world is on the wrong scent in pursuit of happiness. They think it consists in having and getting, and in being served by others. It consists in giving, and in serving others. He that would be great among you, said Christ, let him serve. He that would be happy, let him remember that there is but one way—it is more blessed, it is more happy, to give than to receive.

The next ingredient is a very remarkable one: *Good Temper.* "Love is not easily provoked." Nothing could be more striking than to find this here. We are inclined to look upon bad temper as a very harmless weakness. We speak of it as a mere infirmity of nature, a family failing, a matter of temperament, not a thing to take into very serious account in estimating a man's character. And yet here, right in the heart of this analysis of love, it finds a place; and the Bible again and again returns to condemn it as one of the most destructive elements in human nature.

The peculiarity of ill temper is that it is the vice of the virtuous. It is often the one blot on an otherwise noble character. You know men who are all but perfect, and women who would be entirely perfect, but for an easily ruffled, quick-tempered, or "touchy" disposition. This compatibility of ill temper with high moral character is one of the strangest and saddest problems of ethics. The truth is there are two great classes of sins— sins of the *Body,* and sins of the *Disposition.* The Prodigal Son may be taken as a type of the first, the Elder Brother of the second. Now, society has no doubt whatever as to which of these is the worse. Its brand falls, without a challenge, upon the

Prodigal. But are we right? We have no balance to weigh one another's sins, and coarser and finer are but human words; but faults in the higher nature may be less venial than those in the lower, and to the eye of Him who is Love, a sin against Love may seem a hundred times more base. No form of vice, not worldliness, not greed of gold, not drunkenness itself, does more to un-Christianize society than evil temper. For embittering life, for breaking up communities, for destroying the most sacred relationships, for devastating homes, for withering up men and women, for taking the bloom of childhood, in short, for sheer gratuitous misery-producing power, this influence stands alone. Look at the Elder Brother, moral, hardworking, patient, dutiful—let him get all credit for his virtues —look at this man, this baby, sulking outside his own father's door. "He was angry," we read, "and would not go in." Look at the effect upon the father, upon the servants, upon the happiness of the guests. Judge of the effect upon the Prodigal— and how many prodigals are kept out of the Kingdom of God by the unlovely character of those who profess to be inside? Analyze, as a study in Temper, the thunder-cloud as it gathers upon the Elder-Brother's brow. What is it made of? Jealousy, anger, pride, uncharity, cruelty, self-righteousness, touchiness, doggedness, sullenness,—these are the ingredients of this dark and loveless soul. In varying proportions, also, these are the ingredients of all ill temper. Judge if such sins of the disposition are not worse to live in, and for others to live with, than sins of the body. Did Christ indeed not answer the question Himself when He said, "I say unto you, that the publicans and the harlots go into the Kingdom of Heaven before you"? There is really no place in Heaven for a disposition like this. A man with such a mood could only make Heaven miserable for all the people in it. Except, therefore, such a man be born again, he cannot, he simply *cannot,* enter the Kingdom of Heaven. For it is perfectly certain—and you will not misunderstand me—that to enter Heaven a man must take it with him.

You will see then why Temper is significant. It is not in what it is alone, but in what it reveals. This is why I take the liberty now of speaking of it with such unusual plainness. It is a test for love, a symptom, a revelation of an unloving nature at bottom. It is the intermittent fever which bespeaks unintermittent disease within; the occasional bubble escaping to the surface which betrays some rottenness underneath; a sample of the most hidden products of the soul dropped involuntarily when off one's guard; in a word, the lightning form of a hundred hideous and un-Christian sins. For a want of patience, a want of kindness, a want of generosity, a want of courtesy, a want of unselfishness, all are instantaneously symbolized in one flash of Temper.

Hence it is not enough to deal with the Temper. We must go to the source, and change the inmost nature, and the angry humors will die away of themselves. Souls are made sweet not by taking the acid fluids out, but by putting something in—a great Love, a new Spirit, the Spirit of Christ. Christ, the Spirit of Christ, interpenetrating ours, sweetens, purifies, transforms all. This only can eradicate what is wrong, work a chemical change, renovate and regenerate, and rehabilitate the inner man. Will-power does not change men. Time does not change men. Christ does. Therefore "Let that mind be in you which was also in Christ Jesus." Some of us have not much time to lose. Remember, once more, that this is a matter of life or death. I cannot help speaking urgently, for myself, for yourselves. "Whoso shall offend one of these little ones, which believe in me, it were better for him that a millstone were hanged about his neck, and that he were drowned in the depth of the sea." That is to say, it is the deliberate verdict of the Lord Jesus that it is better not to live than not to love. *It is better not to live than not to love.*

Guilelessness and *Sincerity* may be dismissed almost with a word. Guilelessness is the grace for suspicious people. And the possession of it is the great secret of personal influence. You will find, if you think for a moment, that the people who influence you are people who believe in you. In an atmosphere of suspicion men shrivel up; but in that atmosphere they expand, and find encouragement and educative fellowship. It is a wonderful thing that here and there in this hard, uncharitable world there should still be left a few rare souls who think no evil. This is the great unworldliness. Love "Thinketh no evil," imputes no motive, sees the bright side, puts the best construction on every action. What a delightful state of mind to live in! What a stimulus and benediction even to meet with it for a day! To be trusted is to be saved. And if we try to in-fluence or elevate others, we shall soon see that success is in proportion to their belief of our belief in them. For the respect of another is the first restoration of the self-respect a man has lost; our ideal of what he is becomes to him the hope and pat-tern of what he may become.

"Love rejoiceth not in iniquity, but rejoiceth in the truth." I have called this *Sincerity* from the words rendered in the Authorized Version by "rejoiceth in the truth." And, certainly, were this the real translation, nothing could be more just. For he who loves will love Truth not less than men. He will rejoice in the Truth—rejoice not in what he has been taught to believe; not in this Church's doctrine or in that; not in this ism or in that ism; but "in *the Truth*." He will accept only what is real; he will strive to get at facts; he will search for *Truth* with a humble and unbiased mind, and cherish whatever he finds at any sacrifice. But the more literal translation of the Revised Version calls for just such a sacrifice for truth's sake here. For what Paul really meant is, as we there read, "Rejoiceth not in unrighteousness, but rejoiceth with the truth," a quality which probably no one English word—and certainly not *Sincerity*—adequately defines. It includes, perhaps more strictly, the self-restraint which refuses to make capital out of others' faults; the charity which delights not in exposing the weakness of others, but "covereth all things"; the sincerity of purpose which en-deavors to see things as they are, and rejoices to find them bet-ter than suspicion feared or calumny denounced.

So much for the analysis of Love. Now the business of our lives is to have these things fitted into our characters. That is the supreme work to which we need to address ourselves in this world, to learn Love. Is life not full of opportunities for learning Love? Every man and woman every day has a thou-sand of them. The world is not a playground; it is a school-room. Life is not a holiday, but an education. And the one eter-

nal lesson for us all is *how better we can love.* What makes a
man a good cricketer? Practice. What makes a man a good
artist, a good sculptor, a good musician? Practice. What makes
a man a good linguist, a good stenographer? Practice. What
makes a man a good man? Practice. Nothing else. There is
nothing capricious about religion. We do not get the soul in
different ways, under different laws, from those in which we
get the body and the mind. If a man does not exercise his arm
he develops no biceps muscle; and if a man does not exercise
his soul, he acquires no muscle in his soul, no strength of character, no vigor of moral fibre, nor beauty of spiritual growth.
Love is not a thing of enthusiastic emotion. It is a rich, strong,
manly, vigorous expression of the whole round Christian character—the Christlike nature in its fullest development. And the
constituents of this great character are only to be built up
by ceaseless practice.

What was Christ doing in the carpenter's shop? Practicing.
Though perfect, we read that He *learned* obedience, and grew
in wisdom and in favor with God. Do not quarrel therefore
with your lot in life. Do not complain of its never ceasing cares,
its petty environment, the vexations you have to stand, the
small and sordid souls you have to live and work with. Above
all, do not resent temptation; do not be perplexed because it
seems to thicken round you more and more, and ceases neither
for effort nor for agony nor prayer. That is your practice. That
is the practice which God appoints you; and it is having its
work in making you patient, and humble, and generous, and
unselfish, and kind, and courteous. Do not grudge the hand
that is moulding the still too shapeless image within you. It is
growing more beautiful, though you see it not, and every
touch of temptation may add to its perfection. Therefore keep
in the midst of life. Do not isolate yourself. Be among men, and
among things, and among troubles, and difficulties, and ob-
stacles. You remember Goethe's words: *Es bildet ein Talent
sich in der Stille, Doch ein Charakter in dem Stromder Welt.*
"Talent develops itself in solitude; character in the stream of
life." Talent develops itself in solitude—the talent of prayer,
of faith, of meditation, of seeing the unseen: Character grows

in the stream of the world's life. That chiefly is where men are to learn love.

How? Now, how? To make it easier, I have named a few of the elements of love. But these are only elements. Love itself can never be defined. Light is a something more than the sum of its ingredients—a glowing, dazzling, tremulous ether. And love is something more than all its elements—a palpitating, quivering, sensitive, living thing. By synthesis of all the colors, men can make whiteness, they cannot make light. By synthesis of all the virtues, men can make virtue, they cannot make love. How then are we to have this transcendent living whole conveyed into our souls? We brace our wills to secure it. We try to copy those who have it. We lay down rules about it. We watch. We pray. But these things alone will not bring Love into our nature. Love is an *effect*. And only as we fulfil the right condition can we have the effect produced. Shall I tell you what the *cause* is?

If you turn to the Revised Version of the First Epistle of John you will find these words: "We love because He first loved us." "We love," not "We love *Him*." That is the way the old version has it, and it is quite wrong. "*We love*—because He first loved us." Look at that word "because." It is the *cause* of which I have spoken. "*Because* He first loved us," the effect follows that we love, we love Him, we love all men. We cannot help it. Because He loved us, we love, we love everybody. Our heart is slowly changed. Contemplate the love of Christ, and you will love. Stand before that mirror, reflect Christ's character and you will be changed into the same image from tenderness to tenderness. There is no other way. You cannot love to order. You can only look at the lovely object, and fall in love with it, and grow into likeness to it. And so look at this Perfect Character, this Perfect Life. Look at the great Sacrifice as He laid down Himself, all through life, and upon the Cross of Calvary, and you must love Him. And loving Him, you must become like Him. Love begets love. It is a process of induction. Put a piece of iron in the presence of an electrified body, and that piece of iron for a time becomes electrified. It is changed into a temporary magnet in the mere presence of a permanent magnet, and as long as you leave the two side by side, they are both magnets alike. Remain side by side with Him who loved us, and gave Himself for us, and you too will become a permanent magnet, a permanently attractive force; and like Him you will draw all men unto you, like him you will be drawn unto all men. That is the inevitable effect of Love. Any man who fulfils that cause must have that effect produced in him. Try to give up the idea that religion comes to us by chance, or by mystery, or by caprice. It comes to us by natural law, or by supernatural law, for all law is Divine. Edward Irving went to see a dying boy once, and when he entered the room he just put his hand on the sufferer's head, and said, "My boy, God loves you," and went away. And the boy started from his bed, and called out to the people in the house, "God loves me! God loves me!" It changed that boy. The sense that God loved him overpowered him, melted him down, and began the creating of a new heart in him. And that is how the love of God melts down the unlovely heart in man, and begets in him the new creature, who is patient and humble and gentle and unselfish. And there is no other way to get it. There is no mystery about it. We love others, we love everybody, we love our enemies, because He first loved us.

The Defence

NOW I have a closing sentence or two to add about Paul's reason for singling out love as the supreme possession. It is a very remarkable reason. In a single word it is this: *it lasts.* "Love," urges Paul, "never faileth." Then he begins again one of his marvelous lists of the great things of the day, and exposes them one by one. He runs over the things that men thought were going to last, and shows that they are all fleeting, temporary, passing away.

"Whether there be prophecies, they shall fail." It was the mother's ambition for her boy in those days that he should become a prophet. For hundreds of years God had never spoken by means of any prophet, and at that time the prophet was greater than the King. Men waited wistfully for another messenger to come and hung upon his lips when he appeared as upon the very voice of God. Paul says, "Whether there be prophecies, they shall fail." This book is full of prophecies. One by one they have "failed"; that is, having been fulfilled, their work is finished; they have nothing more to do now in the world except to feed a devout man's faith.

Then Paul talks about tongues. That was another thing that was greatly coveted. "Whether there be tongues, they shall cease." As we all know, many, many centuries have passed since tongues have been known in this world. They have ceased. Take it in any sense you like. Take it, for illustration merely, as languages in general—a sense which was not in Paul's mind at all, and which though it cannot give us the specific lesson will point the general truth. Consider the words in which these chapters were written—Greek. It has gone. Take the Latin—the other great tongue of those days. It ceased long ago. Look at the Indian language. It is ceasing. The language of Wales, of Ireland, of the Scottish Highlands, is dying before our eyes. The most popular book in the English tongue at the present time, except the Bible, is one of Dickens's works, his *Pickwick Papers*. It is largely written in the language of London street-life; and experts assure us that in fifty years it will be unintelligible to the average English reader.

Then Paul goes farther, and with even greater boldness adds, "Whether there be knowledge, it shall vanish away." The wisdom of the ancients, where is it? It is wholly gone. A schoolboy to-day knows more than Sir Isaac Newton knew. His knowledge has vanished away. You put yesterday's newspaper in the fire. Its knowledge has vanished away. You buy the old editions of the great encyclopædias for a few pence. Their knowledge has vanished away. Look how the coach has been superseded by the use of steam. Look how electricity has superseded that, and swept a hundred almost new inventions into oblivion. One of the greatest living authorities, Sir William Thomson, said the other day, "The steam-engine is passing away." "Whether there be knowledge, it shall vanish away." At every workshop you will see, in a back yard, a heap of old iron, a few wheels, a few levers, a few cranks, broken and eaten with rust. Twenty years ago that was the pride of the city. Men flocked in from the country to see the great invention; now it is superseded, its day is done. And all the boasted science and philosophy of this day will soon be old. But yesterday, in the University of Edinburgh, the greatest figure in the faculty was Sir James Simpson, the discoverer of chloroform. The other day his successor and nephew, Professor Simpson, was asked by the librarian of the University to go to the library and pick out the books on his subject that were no longer needed. And his reply to the librarian was this: "Take every text-book that is more than ten years old, and put it down in the cellar." Sir James Simpson was a great authority only a few years ago: men came from all parts of the earth to consult him; and almost the whole teaching of that time is consigned by the science of to-day to oblivion. And in every branch of science it is the same. "Now we know in part. We see through a glass darkly."

Can you tell me anything that is going to last? Many things Paul did not condescend to name. He did not mention money, fortune, fame; but he picked out the great things of his time, the things the best men thought had something in them, and brushed them peremptorily aside. Paul had no charge against these things in themselves. All he said about them was that they would not last. They were great things, but not supreme things. There were things beyond them. What we are stretches past what we do, beyond what we possess. Many things that men denounce as sins are not sins; but they are temporary. And that is a favorite argument of the New Testament. John says of the world, not that it is wrong, but simply that it "passeth away." There is a great deal in the world that is delightful and beautiful; there is a great deal in it that is great and engrossing; but it will not last. All that is in the world, the lust of the eye, the lust of the flesh, and the pride of life, are but for a little while. Love not the world therefore. Nothing that it contains is worth the life and consecration of an immortal soul. The immortal soul must give itself to something that is immortal. And the only immortal things are these: "Now abideth faith, hope, love, but the greatest of these is love."

Some think the time may come when two of these three things will also pass away—faith into sight, hope into fruition. Paul does not say so. We know but little now about the conditions of the life that is to come. But what is certain is that Love must last. God, the Eternal God, is Love. Covet therefore that everlasting gift, that one thing which it is certain is going to stand, that one coinage which will be current in the Universe when all the other coinages of all the nations of the world shall be useless and unhonored. You will give yourselves to many things, give yourself first to Love. Hold things in their proportion. *Hold things in their proportion.* Let at least the first great object of our lives be to achieve the character defended in these words, the character—and it is the character of Christ —which is built round Love.

I have said this thing is eternal. Did you ever notice how continually John associates love and faith with eternal life? I was not told when I was a boy that "God so loved the world that He gave His only-begotten Son, that whosoever believeth in Him should have everlasting life." What I was told, I remember, was, that God so loved the world that, if I trusted in Him, I was to have a thing called peace, or I was to have rest, or I was to have joy, or I was to have safety. But I had to find out for myself that whosoever trusteth in Him—that is, whosoever loveth Him, for trust is only the avenue to Love—hath ever-lasting *life*. The Gospel offers a man life. Never offer men a thimbleful of Gospel. Do not offer them merely joy, or merely peace, or merely rest, or merely safety; tell them how Christ came to give men a more abundant life than they have, a life abundant in love, and therefore abundant in salvation for themselves, and large in enterprise for the alleviation and re-demption of the world. Then only can the Gospel take hold of the whole of a man, body, soul, and spirit, and give to each part of his nature its exercise and reward. Many of the current Gospels are addressed only to a part of man's nature. They of-fer peace, not life; faith, not Love; justification, not regenera-tion. And men slip back again from such religion because it has never really held them. Their nature was not all in it. It offered no deeper and gladder life-current than the life that was lived before. Surely it stands to reason that only a fuller love can compete with the love of the world.

To love abundantly is to live abundantly, and to love for-ever is to live forever. Hence, eternal life is inextricably bound up with love. We want to live forever for the same reason that we want to live to-morrow. Why do you want to live to-morrow? It is because there is some one who loves you, and whom you want to see to-morrow, and be with, and love back. There is no other reason why we should live on than that we love and are beloved. It is when a man has no one to love him that he commits suicide. So long as he has friends, those who love him and whom he loves, he will live, because to live is to love. Be it but the love of a dog, it will keep him in life; but let that go and he has no contact with life, no reason to live. He dies by his own hand. Eternal life also is to know God, and God is love. This is Christ's own definition. Ponder it. "This is life eternal, that they might know Thee the only true God, and Jesus Christ whom Thou hast sent." Love must be eternal. It is what God is. On the last analysis, then, love is life. Love never

faileth, and life never faileth, so long as there is love. That is
the philosophy of what Paul is showing us; the reason why in
the nature of things Love should be the supreme thing—because it is going to last; because in the nature of things it is an
Eternal Life. It is a thing that we are living now, not that we
get when we die; that we shall have a poor chance of getting
when we die unless we are living now. No worse fate can befall
a man in this world than to live and grow old alone, unloving
and unloved. To be lost is to live in an unregenerate condition,
loveless and unloved; and to be saved is to love; and he that
dwelleth in love dwelleth already in God. For God is Love.

Now I have all but finished. How many of you will join me
in reading this chapter once a week for the next three months?
A man did that once and it changed his whole life. Will you do
it? It is for the greatest thing in the world. You might begin by
reading it every day, especially the verses which describe the
perfect character. "Love suffereth long, and is kind; love envieth not; love vaunteth not itself." Get these ingredients into
your life. Then everything that you do is eternal. It is worth
doing. It is worth giving time to. No man can become a saint
in his sleep; and to fulfil the condition required demands a certain amount of prayer and meditation and time, just as im-
provement in any direction, bodily or mental, requires prepa-
ration and care. Address yourselves to that one thing; at any
cost have this transcendent character exchanged for yours. You
will find as you look back upon your life that the moments that
stand out, the moments when you have really lived, are the
moments when you have done things in a spirit of love. As
memory scans the past, above and beyond all the transitory
pleasures of life, there leap forward those supreme hours when
you have been enabled to do unnoticed kindnesses to those
round about you, things too trifling to speak about, but which
you feel have entered into your eternal life. I have seen almost
all the beautiful things God has made; I have enjoyed almost
every pleasure that He has planned for man; and yet as I look
back I see standing out above all the life that has gone four or
five short experiences when the love of God reflected itself in
some poor imitation, some small act of love of mine, and these

seem to be the things which alone of all one's life abide. Everything else in all our lives is transitory. Every other good is visionary. But the acts of love which no man knows about, or can ever know about—they never fail.

In the book of Matthew, where the Judgment Day is depicted for us in the imagery of One seated upon a throne and dividing the sheep from the goats, the test of a man then is not, "How have I believed?" but "How have I loved?" The test of religion, the final test of religion, is not religiousness but Love. I say the final test of religion at that great Day is not religiousness, but Love; not what I have done, not what I have believed, not what I have achieved, but how I have discharged the common charities of life. Sins of commission in that awful indictment are not even referred to. By what we have not done, *by sins of omission,* we are judged. It could not be otherwise. For the withholding of love is the negation of the spirit of Christ, the proof that we never knew Him, that for us He lived in vain. It means that He suggested nothing in all our thoughts, that He inspired nothing in all our lives, that we were not once near enough to Him to be seized with the spell of His compassion for the world. It means that—

> *"I lived for myself, I thought for myself,*
> *For myself, and none beside—*
> *Just as if Jesus had never lived,*
> *As if He had never died."*

It is the Son of *Man* before whom the nations of the world shall be gathered. It is in the presence of *Humanity* that we shall be charged. And the spectacle itself, the mere sight of it, will silently judge each one. Those will be there whom we have met and helped; or there, the unpitied multitude whom we neglected or despised. No other Witness need be summoned. No other charge than lovelessness shall be preferred. Be not deceived. The words which all of us shall one Day hear sound not of theology but of life, not of churches and saints but of the hungry and the poor, not of creeds and doctrines but of shelter and clothing, not of Bibles and prayer-books but of cups of cold water in the name of Christ. Thank God the Christianity of to-day is coming nearer the world's need. Live to help that on. Thank God men know better, by a hair's-breadth, what religion is, what God is, who Christ is, where Christ is. Who is Christ? He who fed the hungry, clothed the naked, visited the sick. And where is Christ? Where?—whoso shall receive a little child in My name receiveth Me. And who are Christ's? Every one that loveth is born of God.

Brother Lawrence

His Conversations and Letters
on the Practice of the
Presence of God

From the Preface to the Original French Edition, A.D. 1692

"Although death has carried off last year many of the Order of the Carmelites Dechausses, brethren who have left in dying rare legacies of lives of virtue; Providence, it would seem, has desired that the eyes of men should be cast chiefly on Brother Lawrence . . .

"Several persons having seen a copy of one of his letters, have desired to see more; and to meet this wish, care has been taken to collect as many as possible of those which Brother Lawrence wrote with his own hand . . .

"All Christians will find herein much that is edifying. Those in the thick of the great world will learn from these letters how greatly they deceive themselves, seeking for peace and joy in the false glitter of the things that are seen, yet temporal: those who are seeking the Highest Good will gain from this book strength to persevere in the practice of virtue. All, whatever their lifework, will find profit, for they will see herein a brother, busied as they are in outward affairs, who in the midst of the most exacting occupations, has learnt so well to accord action with contemplation, that for the space of more than forty years he hardly ever turned from the Presence of God."

FOREWORD

Now when they saw the boldness of Peter and John, and perceived that they were unlearned and ignorant men, they marvelled; and they took knowledge of them, that they had been with Jesus. Acts 4: 13.

The world is used to receiving an endless number of books at the hands of clerkly and learned men—soon to forget or reject most of them as no great loss.

But it has a way of treasuring a certain Fisherman's memories taken down by a bright young companion; or the fortunes of a wayfarer grubbed out on paper by a Tinker twelve years in jail. Peter's *Gospel* and Bunyan's *Pilgrim's Progress* are secure as long as men shall read. And so perhaps is this present little book. Men have been reading it for their good ever since its humble author died just two hundred and fifty years ago.

There must have been something rare in a monastery cook that a Grand Vicar should listen to his talk and go home and make notes of it; and that high-placed persons should beg of him not the recipe for a sauce but his secret of a happy life. This secret, sharp critics may say, is not the whole of wisdom, not a complete system either of philosophy or theology. But even today it is a life-saver to the harried citizen pulled one way by mystery and the other way by matter-of-fact. Your average man will stop and listen to a cook who knows God, when the animadversions of theologians and philosophers only weary him as babblings in a strange tongue.

Brother Lawrence lived in times strangely like our own. He began life as Nicholas Herman in Lorraine—at one of the many alternations when the province was French. In his boyhood began that Thirty Years' War which drew all Europe into its bloody maw—and still has some part in the outraged world of 1941.

No doubt Nicholas Herman was one of millions sucked into that vortex, for first he was a common soldier. Later, he himself tells us "that he had been a footman to Monsieur Fieubert, the treasurer, and that he was a great awkward fellow, who broke everything."

There are all too many of us now past middle age who feel soiled and weary—the bloom rubbed off from our aspirations —our hopes scaled down to the living of a life more mediocre every day. To such it comes like second wind to consort with a man of fifty who takes hold of himself and finds heaven on earth among the pots and pans of an institution's kitchen. We may demure that he was of finer stuff than we; but No, he pleads, I did nothing but let God have His own way with me.

It is in the hope that many will take this bare-footed lay brother at his word, and make his *Practice* their own, that the editor has collated this edition from many of former centuries, and sends it on its way.

Cincinnati, St. James Day, 1941.

Conversations

FIRST CONVERSATION
August 3, 1666

THE first time I saw Brother Lawrence was upon the third of August, 1666. He told me that God had done him a singular favor, in his conversion at the age of eighteen.

That in the winter, seeing a tree stripped of its leaves, and considering that within a little time the leaves would be renewed, and after that the flowers and fruit appear, he received a high view of the providence and power of God, which has never since been effaced from his soul. That this view had perfectly set him loose from the world, and kindled in him such a love for God that he could not tell whether it had increased during the more than forty years he had lived since.

That he had been footman to M. Fieubert, the treasurer, and that he was a great awkward fellow who broke everything.

That he had desired to be received into a monastery, thinking that he would there be made to smart for his awkwardness and the faults he should commit, and so he should sacrifice to God his life, with its pleasures; but that God had disappointed him, he having met with nothing but satisfaction in that state.

That we should establish in ourselves a sense of God's Presence by continually conversing with Him. That it was a shameful thing to quit His conversation to think of trifles and fooleries.

That we should feed and nourish our souls with high notions of God, which would yield us great joy in being devoted to Him.

That we ought to *quicken—i.e.,* to *enliven—our faith.* That

185

it was lamentable we had so little; and that instead of taking *faith* for the rule of their conduct, men amused themselves with trivial devotions which changed daily. That the way of faith was the spirit of the Church, and that it was sufficient to bring us to a high degree of perfection.

That we ought to give ourselves up entirely to God, with regard both to things temporal and spiritual, and seek our satisfaction only in the fulfilling of His will, whether He lead us by suffering or by consolation, for all would be equal to a soul truly resigned. That there was need of fidelity in those times of dryness, or insensibility and irksomeness in prayer, by which God tries our love to Him; that *then* was the time for us to make good and effectual acts of resignation, whereof one alone would oftentimes very much promote our spiritual advancement.

That as for the miseries and sins he heard of daily in the world, he was so far from wondering at them that, on the contrary, he was surprised that there were not more, considering the malice sinners were capable of; that, for his part, he prayed for them; but knowing that God could remedy the mischiefs they did, when He pleased, he gave himself no further trouble.

That to arrive at such resignation as God requires, we should watch attentively over all the passions which mingle as well in spiritual things as in those of a grosser nature; that God would give light concerning those passions to those who truly desire to serve Him. That if this was my design, *viz.*, sincerely to serve God, I might come to him (Brother Lawrence) as often as I pleased, without any fear of being troublesome; but if not, that I ought no more to visit him.

SECOND CONVERSATION

September 28, 1666

That he had always been governed by love, without selfish views; and that having resolved to make the love of God the *end* of all his actions, he had found good reason to be well sat-

isfied with his method. That he was pleased when he could take
up a straw from the ground for the love of God, seeking Him
only, and nothing else, not even His gifts.

That he had been long troubled in mind from a sure belief
that he was lost; that all the men in the world could not have
persuaded him to the contrary; but that he had thus reasoned
with himself about it: *I engaged in a religious life only for the
love of God, and I have endeavored to act only for Him; whatever becomes of me, whether I be lost or saved, I will always
continue to act purely for the love of God. I shall have this
good at least, that till death I shall have done all that is in me
to love Him.* That this trouble of mind had lasted four years,
during which time he had suffered much; but that at last he
had seen that this trouble arose from want of faith, and that
since then he had passed his life in perfect liberty and continual joy. That he had placed his sins betwixt him and God,
as it were to tell Him that he did not deserve His favors, but
that God still continued to bestow them in abundance.

That in order to form a habit of conversing with God continually, and referring all we do to Him, we must at first apply
to Him with some diligence; but that after a little care we
should find His love inwardly excite us to it without any difficulty.

That he expected, after the pleasant days God had given
him, he should have his turn of pain and suffering; but that
he was not uneasy about it, knowing very well that as he could
do nothing of himself, God would not fail to give him the
strength to bear it.

That when an occasion of practising some virtue offered, he
addressed himself to God, saying, *Lord, I cannot do this unless
Thou enablest me;* and that then he received strength more
than sufficient.

That when he had failed in his duty, he simply confessed his
fault, saying to God, *I shall never do otherwise if Thou leavest
me to myself; it is Thou who must hinder my falling, and mend
what is amiss.* That after this he gave himself no further uneasiness about it.

That we ought to act with God in the greatest simplicity,

speaking to Him frankly and plainly, and imploring His assistance in our affairs just as they happen. That God never failed to grant it, as he had often experienced.

That he had been lately sent into Burgundy to buy the provision of wine for the Society, which was a very unwelcome task to him, because he had no turn for business, and because he was lame and could not go about the boat but by rolling himself over the casks. That, however, he gave himself no uneasiness about it, nor about the purchase of the wine. That he said to God, *It was His business he was about,* and that afterwards he found it very well performed. That he had been sent into Auvergne the year before upon the same account; that he could not tell how the matter passed, but that it proved very well.

So, likewise, in his business in the kitchen (to which he had naturally a great aversion), having accustomed himself to do everything there for the love of God, and with prayer, upon all occasions, for His grace to do his work well, he had found everything easy during the fifteen years that he had been employed there.

That he was very well pleased with the post he was now in; but that he was as ready to quit that as the former, since he was always finding pleasure in every condition by doing little things for the love of God.

That with him the *set* times of prayer were not different from other times; that he retired to pray, according to the directions of his Superior, but that he did not want such retirement, nor ask for it, because his greatest business did not divert him from God.

That as he knew his obligation to love God in all things, and as he endeavored so to do, he had no need of a *director* to advise him, but that he needed much a *confessor* to absolve him. That he was very sensible of his faults, but not discouraged by them; that he confessed them to God, but did not plead against Him to excuse them. When he had so done, he peaceably resumed his usual practice of love and adoration.

That in his trouble of mind he had consulted nobody, but knowing only by the light of faith that God was present, he contented himself with directing all his actions to Him, *i.e.*, doing them with a desire to please Him, let what would come of it.

That useless thoughts spoil all; that the mischief began there, but that we ought to reject them as soon as we perceived their impertinence to the matter in hand or to our salvation, and return to our communion with God.

That at the beginning he had often passed his time appointed for prayer in rejecting wandering thoughts and falling back into them. That he could never regulate his devotion by certain methods as some do. That, nevertheless, at first he had *meditated* for some time, but afterwards that went off in a manner he could give no account of.

That all bodily mortifications and other exercises are useless, except as they serve to arrive at the union with God by love; that he had well considered this, and found it the shortest way to go straight to Him by a continual practice of love and doing all things for His sake.

That we ought to make a great difference between the acts of the *understanding* and those of the *will;* that the first were comparatively of little value, and the others, all. That our only business was to love and delight ourselves in God.

That all possible kinds of mortification, if they were devoid of the love of God, could not efface a single sin. That we ought without anxiety to expect the pardon of our sins from the blood of Jesus Christ, laboring simply to love Him with all our hearts. That God seemed to have granted the greatest favors to the greatest sinners, as more signal monuments of His mercy.

That the greatest pains or pleasures of this world were not to be compared with what he had experienced of both kinds in a spiritual state; so that he was careful for nothing and feared nothing, desiring only one thing of God, *viz.*, that he might not offend Him.

That he had no qualms; for, said he, when I *fail* in my duty, I readily acknowledge it, saying, *I am used to do so; I shall never do otherwise if I am left to myself.* If I fail not, then I give God thanks, acknowledging that the strength comes from Him.

THIRD CONVERSATION

November 22, 1666

He told me that the *foundation of the spiritual life* in *him* had been a high notion and esteem of God in faith; which when he had once well conceived, he had no other care but faithfully to reject at once every other thought, *that he might perform all his actions for the love of God.* That when sometimes he had not thought of God for a good while, he did not disquiet himself for it; but after having acknowledged his wretchedness to God, he returned to Him with so much the greater trust in Him as he had found himself wretched through forgetting Him.

That the trust we put in God honors Him much and draws down great graces.

That it was impossible not only that God should deceive, but also that He should long let a soul suffer which is perfectly surrendered to Him, and resolved to endure everything for His sake.

That he had so often experienced the ready succor of Divine Grace upon all occasions, that from the same experience, when he had business to do, he did not think of it beforehand; but when it was time to do it, he found in God, as in a clear mirror, all that was fit for him to do. That of late he had acted thus, without anticipating care; but before the experience above mentioned, he had been full of care and anxiety in his affairs.

That he had no recollection of what things he had done, once they were past, and hardly realized them when he was about them: that on leaving table, he knew not what he had been eating; but that with one single end in view, he did all for the love of God, rendering Him thanks for that He had directed these acts, and an infinity of others throughout his life: he did all very simply, in a manner which kept him ever steadfastly in the loving Presence of God.

When outward business diverted him a little from the thought of God, a fresh remembrance coming from God invested his soul, and so inflamed and transported him that it was difficult for him to restrain himself.

That he was more united to God in his ordinary occupations than when he left them for devotion in retirement, from which he knew himself to issue with much dryness of spirit.

That he expected hereafter some great pain of body or mind; that the worst that could happen to him would be to lose that sense of God which he had enjoyed so long; but that the goodness of God assured him that He would not forsake him utterly, and that He would give him strength to bear whatever evil He permitted to happen to him; and therefore that he feared nothing, and had no occasion to consult with anybody about his soul. That when he had attempted to do it, he had always come away more perplexed; and that as he was conscious of his readiness to lay down his life for the love of God, he had no apprehension of danger. That perfect abandonment to God was the sure way to heaven, a way on which we had always sufficient light for our conduct.

That in the beginning of the spiritual life we ought to be faithful in doing our duty and denying ourselves; but after that, unspeakable pleasures followed. That in difficulties we need only have recourse to Jesus Christ and beg His grace; with that everything became easy.

That many do not advance in the Christian progress because they stick in penances and particular exercises, while they neglect the love of God, which is the *end*. That this appeared plainly by their works, and was the reason why we see so little solid virtue.

That there was need neither of art nor science for going to God, but only a heart resolutely determined to apply itself to nothing but Him, or for *His* sake, and to love Him only.

FOURTH CONVERSATION
November 25, 1667

He discoursed with me very fervently and with great openness of heart, concerning his manner of *going to God,* whereof some part is related already.

He told me that all consists *in one hearty renunciation* of everything which does not lead us to God in order that we may accustom ourselves to a continual conversation with Him, with freedom and in simplicity. That we need only to recognize God intimately present with us, and to address ourselves to Him every moment, that we may beg His assistance for knowing His will in things doubtful, and for rightly performing those which we plainly see He requires of us; offering them to Him before we do them, and giving Him thanks when we have done.

That in this conversation with God we are also employed in praising, adoring, and loving Him unceasingly, for His infinite goodness and perfection.

That without being discouraged on account of our sins, we should pray for His grace with perfect confidence, relying upon the infinite merits of our Lord Jesus Christ. That God never failed to offer us His grace at every action; that he distinctly perceived it, and never failed of it, unless when his thoughts had wandered from a sense of God's Presence, or he had forgotten to ask His assistance.

That God always gave us light in our doubts when we had no other design but to please Him, and to act for His love.

That our sanctification did not depend upon *changing* our works, but in doing that for God's sake which commonly we do for our own. That it was lamentable to see how many people mistook the means for the end, addicting themselves to certain works, which they performed very imperfectly, by reason of their human or selfish regards.

That the most excellent method he had found of going to God was that of *doing our common business* without any view of pleasing men, (Galatians i. 10; Ephesians vi. 5, 6.) and (as far as we are capable) *purely for the love of God.*

That it was a great delusion to think that the times of prayer ought to differ from other times; that we are as strictly obliged to adhere to God by action in the time of action as by prayer in the season of prayer.

That his view of prayer was nothing else but a sense of the Presence of God, his soul being at that time insensible to everything but Divine Love; and that when the appointed times of prayer were past, he found no difference, because he still continued with God, praising and blessing Him with all his might, so that he passed his life in continual joy; yet hoped that God would give him somewhat to suffer when he should have grown stronger.

That we ought, once for all, heartily to put our whole trust in God, and make a full surrender of ourselves to Him, secure that He would not deceive us.

That we ought not to be weary of doing little things for the love of God, who regards not the greatness of the work, but the love with which it is performed. That we should not wonder if, in the beginning, we often failed in our endeavors, but that at last we should gain a habit, which will naturally produce its acts in us, without our care, and to our exceeding great delight.

That the whole substance of religion was faith, hope, and love, by the practice of which we become united to the will of God; that all besides is indifferent, and to be used only as a means that we may arrive at our end, and be swallowed up therein, by faith and love.

That all things are possible to him who *believes;* that they are less difficult to him who *hopes;* that they are more easy to him who *loves,* and still more easy to him who perseveres in the practice of these three virtues.

That the end we ought to propose to ourselves is to become, in this life, the most perfect worshippers of God we can possibly be, as we hope to be through all eternity.

That when we enter upon the spiritual life, we should consider and examine to the bottom what we are. And then we should find ourselves worthy of all contempt, and not deserving indeed the name of Christians; subject to all kinds of misery and numberless accidents, which trouble us and cause perpetual vicissitudes in our health, in our humors, in our internal and external dispositions; in short, persons whom God would humble by many pains and labors, within as well as without. After this we should not wonder that troubles, temptations, oppositions, and contradictions happen to us from men. We ought, on the contrary, to submit ourselves to them, and bear them as long as God pleases, as things highly beneficial to us.

That the greater perfection a soul aspires after, the more dependent it is upon Divine Grace.

The particulars which follow are collected from other accounts of Brother Lawrence.

Being questioned by one of his own Society (to whom he was obliged to open himself) by what means he had attained such an habitual sense of God, he told him that, since his first coming to the monastery, he had considered God as the *end* of all his thoughts and desires, as the mark to which they should tend, and in which they should terminate.

That in the beginning of his novitiate he spent the hours appointed for private prayer in thinking of God, so as to convince his mind of, and to impress deeply upon his heart, the Divine existence, rather by devout sentiments, and submission to the lights of faith, than by studied reasonings and elaborate meditations. That by this short and sure method he exercised himself in the knowledge and love of God, resolving to use his utmost endeavor to live in a continual sense of His Presence, and, if possible, never to forget Him more.

That when he had thus in prayer filled his mind with great sentiments of that Infinite Being, he went to his work appointed in the kitchen (for he was cook to the Society). There having first considered severally the things his office required, and when and how each thing was to be done, he spent all the intervals of his time, as well before as after his work, in prayer.

That when he began his business, he said to God, with a filial trust in Him: *O my God, since Thou art with me, and I must now, in obedience to Thy commands, apply my mind*

*to these outward things, I beseech Thee to grant me the grace
to continue in Thy Presence; and to this end do Thou prosper
me with Thy assistance, receive all my works, and possess all
my affections.*

["We can do *little* things for God. I turn the cake that is fry-
ing on the pan for love of Him, and that done, if there is nothing else to call me, I prostrate myself in worship before Him,
who has given me grace to work; afterwards I rise happier
than a king. It is enough for me to pick up but a straw from
the ground for the love of God."]

As he proceeded in his work he continued his familiar conversation with his Maker, imploring His grace, and offering
to Him all his actions.

When he had finished he examined himself how he had discharged his duty; if he found *well*, he returned thanks to God;
if otherwise, he asked pardon; and without being discouraged,
he set his mind right again, and continued his exercise of the
Presence of God, as if he had never deviated from it. "Thus,"
said he, "by rising after my falls, and by frequently renewed
acts of faith and love, I am come to a state wherein it would be
as difficult for me not to think of God as it was at first to accustom myself to it."

As Brother Lawrence had found such comfort and blessing
in walking in the Presence of God, it was natural for him to
recommend it earnestly to others; but his example was a
stronger inducement than any arguments he could propose.
His very countenance was edifying; such a sweet and calm
devotion appearing in it as could not but affect all beholders.
And it was observed that in the greatest hurry of business in
the kitchen, he still reserved his recollection and heavenly-
mindedness. He was never hasty nor loitering, but did each
thing in its season, with an even, uninterrupted composure
and tranquillity of spirit. "The time of business," said he, "does
not with me differ from the time of prayer, and in the noise
and clatter of my kitchen, while several persons are at the
same time calling for different things, I possess God in as great
tranquillity as if I were upon my knees at the Blessed Sacra-
ment."

Letters

FIRST LETTER

My Reverend Mother: Since you desire so earnestly that I should communicate to you the method by which I arrived at that *habitual sense of God's Presence,* which our Lord, of His mercy, has been pleased to vouchsafe to me, I must tell you that it is with great difficulty that I am prevailed on by your importunities; and now I do it only upon the terms that you show my letter to nobody. If I knew that you would let it be seen, all the desire that I have for your perfection would not be able to determine me to it.

The account I can give you is this.

Having found in many books different methods of going to God, and divers practices of the spiritual life, I thought this would serve rather to puzzle me than facilitate what I sought after, which was nothing else than how to become wholly God's. This made me resolve to give the *all* for the *all;* so after having given myself wholly to God, to make all the satisfaction I could for my sins, *I renounced, for the love of Him, everything that was not His, and I began to live as if there was none but He and I in the world.* Sometimes I considered myself before Him as a poor criminal at the feet of his judge; at other times I beheld Him in my heart as my Father, as my God. I worshipped Him the oftenest that I could, keeping my mind in His holy Presence, and recalling it as often as I found it wandering from Him. I found no small trouble in this exercise, and yet I continued it, notwithstanding all the difficulties that I encountered, without troubling or disquieting myself when my mind had wandered involuntarily. I made this my business as much all the day long as at the appointed times of prayer;

for at all times, every hour, every minute, even in the height of my business, I drove away from my mind everything that was capable of interrupting my thought of God.

Such has been my common practice ever since I entered monastic life; and though I have done it very imperfectly, yet I have found great advantages by it. These, I well know, are to be imputed solely to the mercy and goodness of God, because we can do nothing without Him, and *I* still less than any. But when we are faithful to keep ourselves in His holy Presence, and set Him always before us, this not only hinders our offending Him and doing anything that may displease Him, at least wilfully, but it also begets in us a holy freedom, and, if I may so speak, a familiarity with God, wherewith we ask, and that successfully, the graces we stand in need of. In short, by often repeating these acts, they become *habitual,* and the *Presence of God* is rendered as it were *natural* to us. Give Him thanks, if you please, with me, for His great goodness toward me, which I can never sufficiently marvel at, for the many favors He has done to so miserable a sinner as I am. May all things praise Him. Amen.

I am, in our Lord, Yours, ——

SECOND LETTER

My Reverend Mother: I have taken this opportunity to communicate to you the thoughts of one of our Society, concerning the wonderful effect and continual succor which he receives from *the Presence of God.* Let you and me both profit by them.

You must know that during the forty years and more that he has spent in religion, his continual care has been to be *always with God;* and to do nothing, say nothing, and think nothing which may displease Him, and this without any other view than purely for the love of Him, and because He deserves infinitely more.

He is now so accustomed to that *Divine Presence* that he receives from it continual succor upon all occasions. For above thirty years his soul has been filled with joys so continual, and sometimes so transcendent, that he is forced to use means to moderate them, and to prevent their appearing outwardly.

If sometimes he is a little too much absent from the *Divine Presence*, which happens often when he is most engaged in his outward business, God presently makes Himself felt in his soul to recall him. He answers with exact fidelity to these inward drawings, either by an elevation of his heart toward God, or by a meek and loving regard to Him; or by such words as love forms upon these occasions, as for instance, *My God, behold me, wholly Thine: Lord, make me according to Thy heart.* And then it seems to him (as in effect he feels it) that this God of love, satisfied with such few words, reposes again, and rests in the depth and center of his soul. The experience of these things gives him such an assurance that God is always deep within his soul, that no doubt of it can arise, whatever may betide.

Judge from this what contentment and satisfaction he enjoys, feeling continually within him so great a treasure. No longer is he in anxious search after it, but he has it open before him, free to take of it what he pleases.

He complains much of our blindness, and exclaims often that we are to be pitied who content ourselves with so little. *God's treasure,* he says, *is like an infinite ocean, yet a little wave of feeling, passing with the moment, contents us. Blind as we are, we hinder God and stop the current of His graces. But when He finds a soul permeated with a living faith, He pours into it His graces and favors plenteously; into the soul they flow like a torrent which, after being forcibly stopped against its ordinary course, when it has found a passage, spreads with impetuosity its pent-up flood.*

Yes, we often stop this torrent by the little value we set upon it. But let us stop it no longer; let us enter into ourselves and break down the barrier which holds it back. Let us make the most of the day of grace; let us redeem the time that is lost, for perhaps we have but little left. Death follows us close; let us be well prepared for it; for we die but once, and a miscarriage *then* is irretrievable.

I say again, let us enter into ourselves. Time presses, there is no room for delay; our souls are at stake. You, I believe, have taken such effectual measures that you will not be surprised. I commend you for it; it is the one thing needful. We must, nevertheless, always work at it, for, in the spiritual life, not to advance is to go back. But those whose spirits are stirred by the breath of the Holy Spirit go forward even in sleep. If the vessel of our soul is still tossed with winds and storms, let us awake the Lord, who reposes in it, and He will quickly calm the sea.

I have taken the liberty to impart to you these good thoughts, that you may compare them with your own. It will serve again to rekindle and inflame them, if by misfortune (which God forbid, for it would be indeed a great misfortune) they should be, though never so little, cooled. Let us then *both* recall our early fervor. Let us profit by the example and thoughts of this brother, who is little known of the world, but known of God, and abundantly blessed by Him. I will pray for you; do you pray instantly for me. I am, in our Lord,

Yours, ——

June 1, 1682

THIRD LETTER

My Reverend and Greatly Honored Mother: I have received today two books and a letter from Sister ——, who is preparing to make her "profession," and upon that account desires the prayers of your holy Community, and yours in particular. I perceive that she reckons much upon them; pray do not disappoint her. Beg of God that she may make her sacrifice in the view of His love alone, and with firm resolution to be wholly devoted to Him. I will send you one of these books, which treat of *the Presence of God,* a subject which in my opinion contains the whole spiritual life; and it seems to me that whoever duly practises it will soon become spiritual.

I know that for the right practice of it the heart must be

empty of all else, because God wills to possess the heart *alone;* and as He cannot possess it *alone* unless it be empty of all besides, so He cannot work in it what He would, unless it be left vacant to Him.

There is not in the world a kind of life more sweet and delightful than that of a continual walk with God. Those only can comprehend it who practise and experience it; yet I do not advise you to do it from that motive. It is not pleasure which we ought to seek in this exercise; but let us do it from the motive of love, and because God would have us so walk.

Were I a preacher, I should, above all other things, preach *the practice of the Presence of God;* and were I a "director," I should advise all the world to do it, so necessary do I think it, and so easy, too.

Ah! knew we but the need we have of the grace and assistance of God, we should never lose sight of Him—no, not for a moment. Believe me; this very instant, make a holy and firm resolution nevermore wilfully to stray from Him, and to live the rest of your days *in His sacred Presence,* for love of Him surrendering, if He think fit, all other pleasures.

Set heartily about this work, and if you perform it as you ought, be assured that you will soon find the effects of it. I will assist you with my prayers, poor as they are. I commend myself earnestly to yours and those of your holy Community, being theirs, and more particularly

Yours, ——

1685

FOURTH LETTER

To the Same: I have received from Mdlle. —— the things which you gave her for me. I wonder that you have not given me your thoughts on the little book I sent to you, and which you must have received. Pray, set heartily about the practice of it in your old age; it is better late than never.

I cannot imagine how religious persons can live satisfied

without *the practice of the Presence of God*. For my part, I keep myself retired with Him in the very center of my soul as much as I can; and while I am so with Him I fear nothing, but the least turning away from Him is to me insupportable.

This exercise does not much fatigue the body; yet it is proper to deprive it sometimes, nay often, of many little pleasures which are innocent and lawful, for God will not permit that a soul which desires to be devoted entirely to Him should take other pleasures than with Him: that is more than reasonable.

I do not say that therefore we must put any violent constraint upon ourselves. No, we must serve God in a holy freedom; we must do our business faithfully, without trouble or disquiet, recalling our mind to God meekly, and with tranquillity, as often as we find it wandering from Him.

It is, however, necessary to put our whole trust in God, laying aside all other cares, and even some particular forms of devotion, though very good in themselves, yet such as one often engages in unreasonably, because these devotions are only means to attain to the end. So when by this *practice of the Presence of God* we are *with Him* who is *our End,* it is then useless to return to the means. Then it is that abiding in His holy Presence, we may continue our commerce of love, now by an act of adoration, of praise, or of desire; now by an act of sacrifice or of thanksgiving, and in all the manners which our mind can devise.

Be not discouraged by the repugnance which you may find to it from nature; you must do yourself violence. Often, at the onset, one thinks it is lost time; but you must go on, and resolve to persevere in it till death, notwithstanding all the difficulties that may occur. I commend myself to the prayers of your holy Community, and to yours in particular. I am, in our Lord,

Yours, ——

November 3, 1685

FIFTH LETTER

Madame: I pity you much. It will be of great importance if you can leave the care of your affairs to M. and Mme. ——, and spend the remainder of your life only in worshipping God. He lays no great burden upon us: a little remembrance of Him from time to time; a little adoration; sometimes to pray for His grace, sometimes to offer Him your sorrows, and sometimes to return Him thanks for the benefits He has given you, and still gives you, in the midst of your troubles. He asks you to console yourself with Him the oftenest you can. Lift up your heart to Him even at your meals and when you are in company; the least little remembrance will always be acceptable to Him. You need not cry very loud; He is nearer to us than we think.

To be with God, there is no need to be continually in church. We may make an oratory of our heart wherein to retire from time to time to converse with Him in meekness, humility, and love. Every one is capable of such familiar conversation with God, some more, some less. He knows what we can do. Let us begin, then. Perhaps He is just waiting for one generous resolution on our part. Have courage. We have but little time to live; you are near sixty-four, and I am almost eighty. Let us live and die with God. Sufferings will be sweet and pleasant to us while we are with Him; and without Him, the greatest pleasures will be anguish to us. May He be blessed for all. Amen.

Accustom yourself, then, by degrees thus to worship Him, to beg His grace, to offer Him your heart from time to time in the midst of your business, even every moment, if you can. Do not scrupulously confine yourself to fixed rules, or particular forms of devotion, but act with faith in God, with love and humility. You may assure M. and Mme. and Mdlle. —— of my poor prayers, and that I am their servant, and particularly
                                          Yours in our Lord, ——

SIXTH LETTER

My Reverend Father: Not finding my manner of life in books, although I have no difficulty about it, yet, for greater security, I shall be glad to know your thoughts concerning it.

In a conversation some days since with a person of piety, he told me that the spiritual life was a life of grace, which begins with servile fear, which is increased by hope of eternal life, and which is consummated by pure love; that each of these states had its different stages, by which one arrives at last at that blessed consummation.

I have not followed all these methods. On the contrary, from I know not what instincts, I found that they discouraged me. This was the reason why, at my entrance into religion, I resolved to give myself up to God as the best satisfaction I could make for my sins, and for the love of Him to renounce all besides.

For the first years I commonly employed myself during the time set apart for devotion with the thought of death, judgment, heaven, hell, and my sins. Thus I continued some years, applying my mind carefully the rest of the day, and even in the midst of my business, *to the Presence of God,* whom I considered always as *with* me, often as *in* me.

At length I came insensibly to do the same thing during my set time of prayer, which caused in me great delight and consolation. This practice produced in me so high an esteem for God that *faith* alone was capable to satisfy me in that point.

Such was my beginning; and yet I must tell you that for the first ten years I suffered much. The apprehension that I was not devoted to God as I wished to be, my past sins always present to my mind, and the great unmerited favors which God bestowed on me, were the matter and source of my sufferings. During this time I fell often, yet as often rose again. It seemed to me that all creation, reason, and God Himself were against me, and *faith* alone for me. I was troubled sometimes with thoughts that to be believe I had received such favors was an effect of my presumption, which pretended to be *at once* where others arrive only with difficulty; at other times, that it was a wilful delusion, and that there was no salvation for me.

When I thought of nothing but to end my days in these times of trouble and disquiet (which did not at all diminish the trust I had in God, and which served only to increase my faith), I found myself changed all at once; and my soul, which till that time was in trouble, felt a profound inward peace, as if it had found its center and place of rest.

Ever since that time I walk before God in simple faith, with humility and with love, and I apply myself diligently to do nothing and think nothing which may displease Him. I hope that when I have done what I can, He will do with me what He pleases.

As for what passes in me at present, I cannot express it. I have no pain nor any doubt as to my state, because I have no will but that of God, which I endeavor to carry out in all things, and to which I am so submissive that I would not take up a straw from the ground against His order, or from any other motive than purely that of love to Him.

I have quitted all forms of devotion and set prayers but those to which my state obliges me. And I make it my only business to persevere is His holy Presence, wherein I keep myself by a simple attention and an absorbing passionate regard to God, which I may call an *actual Presence of God;* or, to speak better, a silent and secret conversation of the soul with God . . .

If sometimes my thoughts wander from it by necessity or infirmity, I am soon recalled by inward emotions so charming and delightful that I am confused to mention them. I beg you to reflect rather upon my great wretchedness, of which you are fully informed, than upon the great favors which God does me, all unworthy and ungrateful as I am.

As for my set hours of prayer, they are only a continuation of the same exercise. Sometimes I consider myself there as a stone before a carver, whereof he is to make a statue; presenting myself thus before God, I desire Him to form His perfect image in my soul, and make me entirely like Himself.

At other times, when I apply myself to prayer I feel all my spirit and all my soul lift itself up without any trouble or effort of mine, and it remains as it were in elevation, fixed firm in God as in its center and its resting-place.

I know that some charge this state with inactivity, delusion, and self-love. I confess that it is a holy inactivity, and would be a happy self-love were the soul in that state capable of such; because, in fact, while the soul is in this repose, it cannot be troubled by such acts as it was formerly accustomed to, and which were then its support, but which would now rather injure than assist it.

Yet I cannot bear that this should be called delusion, because the soul which thus enjoys God desires herein nothing but Him. If this be delusion in me, it belongs to God to remedy it. May He do with me what He pleases; I desire only Him, and to be wholly devoted to Him. You will, however, oblige me in sending me your opinion, to which I always pay a great deference, for I have a singular esteem for your Reverence, and am, in our Lord, my Reverend Father,

Yours, ——

SEVENTH LETTER

My Reverend and Greatly Honored Mother: My prayers, of little worth though they be, will not fail you; I have promised it, and I will keep my word. How happy we might be, if only we could find the Treasure, of which the Gospel tells us—all else would seem to us nothing. How infinite it is! The more one toils and searches in it, the greater are the riches that one finds. Let us toil therefore unceasingly in this search, and let us not grow weary and leave off, till we have found . . .

I know not what I shall become: it seems to me that peace of soul and repose of spirit descend on me, even in sleep. To be without the sense of this peace would be affliction indeed;

but with this calm in my soul even for purgatory I would console myself.

I know not what God purposes with me, or keeps me for; I am in a calm so great that I fear nought. What can I fear, when I am with Him? And with Him, in His Presence, I hold myself the most I can. May all things praise Him. Amen.

Yours, ——

EIGHTH LETTER

Madame: We have a God who is infinitely gracious and knows all our wants. I always thought that He would reduce you to extremity. He will come in His own time, and when you least expect it. Hope in Him more than ever; thank Him with me for the favors He does you, particularly for the fortitude and patience which He gives you in your afflictions. It is a plain mark of the care He takes of you. Comfort yourself, then, with Him, and give thanks for all.

I admire also the fortitude and bravery of M. ——. God has given him a good disposition and a good will; but there is in him still a little of the world and a great deal of youth. I hope the affliction which God has sent him will prove a wholesome medicine to him, and make him take stock of himself. It is an accident which should engage him to put all his trust in *Him* who accompanies him everywhere. Let him think of Him as often as he can, especially in the greatest dangers. A little lifting up of the heart suffices. A little remembrance of God, one act of inward worship, though upon a march and sword in hand, are prayers which, however short, are nevertheless very acceptable to God; and far from lessening a soldier's courage in occasions of danger, they best serve to fortify it.

Let him think then of God the most he can. Let him accustom himself, by degrees, to this small but holy exercise. No one will notice it, and nothing is easier than to repeat often in the day these little acts of inward worship. Recommend to him, if you please, that he think of God the most he can, in the manner here directed. It is very fit and most necessary for a soldier, who is daily in danger of his life, and often of his salvation. I hope that God will assist him and all the family, to whom I present my service, being theirs and in particular

Yours, ——

October 12, 1688

NINTH LETTER
(*Concerning Wandering Thoughts in Prayer*)

My Reverend and Greatly Honored Mother: You tell me nothing new; you are not the only one that is troubled with wandering thoughts. Our mind is extremely roving; but, as the will is mistress of all our faculties, she must recall them, and carry them to God as their last End.

When the mind, for lack of discipline when first we engaged in devotion, has contracted certain bad habits of wandering and dissipation, such habits are difficult to overcome, and commonly draw us, even against our wills, to things of the earth.

I believe one remedy for this is to confess our faults and to humble ourselves before God. I do not advise you to use multiplicity of words in prayer; many words and long discourses being often the occasions of wandering. Hold yourself in prayer before God like a poor, dumb, paralytic beggar at a rich man's gate. Let it be *your business* to keep your mind in *the Presence of the Lord.* If it sometimes wanders and withdraws itself from Him, do not much disquiet yourself for that: trouble and disquiet serve rather to distract the mind than to recall it; the will must bring it back in tranquillity. If you persevere with your whole strength, God will have pity on you.

One way to recall the mind easily in the time of prayer, and preserve it more in tranquillity, is *not to let it wander too far at other times.* You should keep it strictly in *the Presence of*

God; and being accustomed to think of Him often, you will find it easy to keep your mind calm in the time of prayer, or at least to recall it from its wanderings.

I have told you already at large, in my former letters, of the advantages we may draw from this *practice of the Presence of God.* Let us set about it seriously, and pray for one another.

Yours, ——

TENTH LETTER

To the Same: The inclosed is an answer to that which I received from our good Sister ——; pray deliver it to her. She seems to me full of good will, but she wants to go faster than grace. One does not become holy all at once. I commend her to you; we ought to help one another by our advice, and still more by our good examples. You will oblige me by letting me hear of her from time to time, and whether she be very fervent and very obedient.

Let us thus think often that our only business in this life is to please God, and that all besides is perhaps but folly and vanity. You and I have lived a monastic life more than forty years. Have we employed those years in loving and serving God who by His mercy has called us to this state, and for that very end? I am filled with shame and confusion when I reflect, on one hand, upon the great favors which God has bestowed and is still bestowing upon me; and, on the other, upon the ill use I have made of them, and my small advancement in the way of perfection.

Since by His mercy He gives us still a little time, let us begin in earnest; let us repair the lost time; let us return with a whole-hearted trust to that *Father of mercies,* who is always ready to receive us into His loving arms. Let us renounce and renounce generously, with single heart, for the love of Him, all that is not His; He deserves infinitely more. Let us think of Him perpetually. Let us put all our trust in Him. I doubt not but that we shall soon find the effects of it in receiving the abundance of His grace, with which we can do all things, and without which we can do nothing but sin.

We cannot escape the dangers which abound in life without the actual and *continual* help of God. Let us, then, pray to Him for it *continually*. How can we pray to Him without being with Him? How can we be with Him but in thinking of Him often? And how can we often think of Him unless by a holy habit of thought which we should form? You will tell me that I am always saying the same thing. It is true, for this is the best and easiest method I know; and as I use no other, I advise all the world to do it. We must *know* before we can *love*. In order to *know* God, we must often *think* of Him; and when we come to *love* Him, we shall then also think of Him often, for our heart will be with our treasure. This is an argument which well deserves your consideration.

I am, Yours, ——

March 28, 1689

ELEVENTH LETTER

Madame: I have had a good deal of difficulty to bring myself to write to M. ——, and I do it now purely because you and Mme. —— desire me. Pray write the directions and send it to him. I am very well pleased with the trust which you have in God; I wish that He may increase it in you more and more. We cannot have too much confidence in so good and faithful a Friend, who will never fail us in this world or the next.

If M. —— knows how to profit by the loss he has had, and puts all his confidence in God, He will soon give him another friend, more powerful and more inclined to serve him. He disposes of hearts as He pleases. Perhaps M. —— was too much attached to him he has lost. We ought to love our friends, but without encroaching upon our chief love which is due to God.

Remember, I pray you, what I have often recommended, which is, to think often on God, by day, by night, in your business, and even in your diversions. He is always near you and with you; leave Him not alone. You would think it rude to leave a friend alone who came to visit you; why, then, must God be neglected? Do not, then, forget Him, but think on Him often, adore Him continually, live and die with Him; this is the glorious employment of a Christian. In a word, this is our profession; if we do not know it, we must learn it. I will endeavor to help you with my prayers, and am, in our Lord,

Yours, ——

October 29, 1689

TWELFTH LETTER

My Reverend and Greatly Honored Mother: I do not pray that you may be delivered from your troubles, but I pray God earnestly that He would give you strength and patience to bear them as long as He pleases. Comfort yourself with Him who holds you fastened to the cross. He will loose you when He thinks fit. Happy those who suffer with Him. Accustom yourself to suffer in that manner, and seek from Him the strength to endure as much and as long as He shall judge to be necessary for you. The men of the world do not comprehend these truths, nor is it to be wondered at, since they suffer as lovers of the world, and not as lovers of Christ. They consider sickness as a pain of nature, and not as from God; and seeing it only in that light, they find nothing in it but grief and distress. But those who consider sickness as coming from the hand of God, as the effect of His mercy, and the means which He employs for their salvation—such commonly find in it great consolation.

I wish you could convince yourself that God is often nearer to us, and more effectually present with us, in sickness than in health. Rely upon no other physician; for, according to my apprehension, He reserves your cure to Himself. Put, then, all your trust in Him, and you will soon find the effects of it in your recovery, which we often retard by putting greater confidence in medicine than in God.

Whatever remedies you make use of, they will succeed only so far as He permits. When pains come from God, He alone can cure them. He often sends diseases of the body to cure those of the soul. Comfort yourself with the sovereign Physician both of the soul and body.

I foresee that you will tell me that I am very much at my ease, that I eat and drink at the table of the Lord. You are right: but think you that it would be a small pain to the greatest criminal in the world to eat at his king's table and to be served by his king's hands, without however being assured of pardon? I believe that he would feel exceeding great uneasiness, and such as nothing could moderate, save only his trust in the goodness of his sovereign. So I can assure you that whatever pleasures I taste at the table of my King, my sins ever present before my eyes, as well as the uncertainty of my pardon, torment me: though in truth, that torment itself is pleasing.

Be satisfied with the state in which God places you; however happy you may think me, I envy you. Pains and sufferings would be a paradise to me while I should suffer with my God, and the greatest pleasures would be a hell to me if I could relish them without Him. All my joy would be to suffer something for His sake.

I must, in a little time, go to God. What comforts me in this life is that I now see Him by *faith;* and I see Him in such a manner as might make me say sometimes, *I believe no more, but I see.* I feel what faith teaches us, and in that assurance and that practice of faith I will live and die with Him.

Continue, then, always with God; it is the only support and comfort for your affliction. I shall beseech Him to be with you. I present my service to the Reverend Mother Superior, and commend myself to your prayers, and am, in our Lord,

Yours, ——

November 17, 1690

THIRTEENTH LETTER

My Good Mother: If we were well accustomed to the exercise of *the Presence of God*, all bodily diseases would be much alleviated thereby. God often permits that we should suffer a little to purify our souls and oblige us to continue *with Him*. I cannot understand how a soul, which is with God and which desires Him alone, can feel pain: I have had enough experience to banish all doubt that it can.

Take courage; offer Him your pains unceasingly; pray to Him for strength to endure them. Above all, acquire a habit of conversing often with God, and forget Him the least you can. Adore Him in your infirmities, offer yourself to Him from time to time, and in the very height of your sufferings beseech Him humbly and affectionately (as a child his good father) to grant you the aid of His grace and to make you conformable to His holy will. I shall endeavor to help you with my poor halting prayers.

God has many ways of drawing us to Himself. He sometimes hides Himself from us; but *faith* alone, which will not fail us in time of need, ought to be our support, and the foundation of our confidence, which must be all in God.

I know not how God will dispose of me. Happiness grows upon me. The whole world suffers; yet I, who deserve the severest discipline, feel joys so continual and so great that I can scarce contain them.

I would willingly ask of God a share of your sufferings, but that I know my weakness, which is so great that if He left me one moment to myself I should be the most wretched man alive. And yet I know not how He can leave me alone, because faith gives me as strong a conviction as sense can do that He never forsakes us until we have first forsaken Him. Let us fear to leave Him. Let us be always with Him. Let us live and die in His Presence. Do you pray for me as I for you.

I am, Yours, ——

November 28, 1690

FOURTEENTH LETTER

To the Same: I am in pain to see you suffer so long. What gives me some ease and sweetens the sorrow I have for your griefs is that I am convinced that they are tokens of God's love for you. Look at them in this light and you will bear them more easily. As your case is, it is my opinion that you should leave off human remedies, and resign yourself entirely to the providence of God. Perhaps He stays only for that resignation and a perfect trust in Him to cure you. Since, notwithstanding all your cares, medicine has hitherto proved unsuccessful, and your malady still increases, it will not be tempting God to abandon yourself into His hands and expect all from Him.

I told you in my last that He sometimes permits the body to suffer to cure the sickness of the soul. Have courage, then; make a virtue of necessity. Ask of God, not deliverance from the body's pains, but strength to bear resolutely, for the love of Him, all that He should please, and as long as He shall desire.

Such prayers, indeed, are a little hard to nature, but most acceptable to God, and sweet to those that love Him. Love sweetens pain; and when one loves God, one suffers for His sake with joy and courage. Do you so, I beseech you; comfort yourself with Him, who is the only Physician of all our ills. He is the Father of the afflicted, always ready to help us. He loves us infinitely, more than we imagine. Love Him, then, and seek no other relief than in Him. I hope you will soon receive it. Adieu. I will help you with my prayers, poor as they are, and shall always be, in our Lord,

Yours, ——

FIFTEENTH LETTER

To the Same: I render thanks to our Lord for having relieved you a little, according to your desire. I have been often near expiring, but I never was so much satisfied as then. Accordingly, I did not pray for any relief, but I prayed for strength to suffer with courage, humility, and love. Ah, how sweet it is to suffer with God! However great the sufferings may be, receive them with love. It is paradise to suffer and be with Him; so that if even now in this life we would enjoy the peace of paradise, we must accustom ourselves to a familiar, humble, affectionate conversation with Him. We must prevent our spirits' wandering from Him upon any occasion. We must make our heart a spiritual temple, wherein to adore Him unceasingly. We must watch continually over ourselves, that we may not do nor say nor think anything that may displease Him. When our minds are thus filled with God, suffering will become full of sweetness, and of quiet joy.

I know that to arrive at this state the beginning is very difficult, for we must act purely in faith. But though it is difficult, we know also that we can do all things with the grace of God, which He never refuses to them who ask it earnestly. Knock, keep on knocking, and I answer for it that He will open to you in His due time, and grant you all at once what He has deferred many years. Adieu. Pray to Him for me as I pray to Him for you. I hope to see Him very soon.

I am, Yours, ——

January 22, 1691

SIXTEENTH LETTER

To the Same: God knoweth best what is needful for us, and all that He does is for our good. If we knew how much He loves us, we should always be ready to receive equally and with indifference from His hand the sweet and the bitter. All would please that came from Him. The sorest afflictions never appear intolerable, except when we see them in the wrong light. When we see them as dispensed by the hand of God, when we know that it is our loving Father who abases and distresses us, our sufferings lose all their bitterness and our mourning becomes all joy.

Let all our business be to *know* God; the more one *knows* Him, the more one *desires* to know Him. And as *knowledge* is commonly the measure of *love,* the deeper and more extensive our *knowledge* shall be, the greater will be our *love;* and if our love of God be great, we shall love Him equally in grief and in joy.

Let us not content ourselves with loving God for the mere sensible favors, how elevated so ever, which He has done or may do us. Such favors, though never so great, cannot bring us so near to Him as faith does in one simple act. Let us seek Him often by faith. He is within us; seek Him not elsewhere. If we do love Him alone, are we not rude, and do we not deserve blame, if we busy ourselves about trifles which do not please and perhaps offend Him? It is to be feared these *trifles* will one day cost us dear.

Let us begin to be devoted to Him in good earnest. Let us cast everything besides out of our hearts. He would possess them alone. Beg this favor of Him. If we do what we can on our parts, we shall soon see that change wrought in us which we aspire after. I cannot thank Him sufficiently for the relief He has vouchsafed you. I hope from His mercy the favor of seeing Him within a few days.* Let us pray for one another.

I am, in our Lord, Yours, ——

February 6, 1691

* He took to his bed two days after, and died within the week.

Reprinted by permission from "Practice and Presence of God," published by The Forward Movement Publications, 412 Sycamore St., Cincinnati, Ohio.

Vital Books That Have Helped the Author

THE TRUE CHRISTIAN RELIGION by Emanuel Swedenborg—This is one of the greatest books on religion since the writing of the Bible. It provides a clear, concise reading of the teachings he gave to the world in a form suitable to every thinking person. It possesses universal appeal for all, of any religion.

OPEN THE DOOR by Wilfred Brandon, transcribed by Edith Ellis— Wilfred Brandon, living in our next life, in the world of spirits, guided Edith Ellis' hand in New York to transcribe automatically how we pass through death and find we have not died and how we live in our next life.

INCARNATION by Wilfred Brandon, transcribed by Edith Ellis—Gives for the first time an explanation of the evolution of the soul and the differing methods of incarnation. It also sets forth in simple terms the process of the soul's emergence and adjustment on the Etheric Plane.

WE KNEW THESE MEN by Wilfred Brandon, transcribed by Edith Ellis—This work is colossal in importance. It relates the experiences of a group of soldiers, killed in war, that arrives on the Etheric Plane. Brandon reports their bewilderment and gradual adjustment. He got to know the loved ones they left behind and how they were able to establish communication with friends and relatives on the earthly plane.

YOUR MIND CAN HEAL YOU by Frederick W. Bailes—Dr. Bailes was able to heal himself of diabetes. By applying a definite Law of Mental Healing, which can be applied by anyone, he was able to heal others of T.B., stomach ulcers, eczema, migraine headaches, sinus afflictions, arthritis, etc.

THE HEALING LIGHT by Agnes Sanford—In this amazing book Mrs. Sanford tells how she heals by the laying on of the hands as Jesus did. She has done many miracles in healing. And she tells how to get faith without which healing is impossible. Her book explains secrets of healing we never understood before.

THERE IS A RIVER by Thomas Sugrue—This work tells the actual, verified history of Edgar Cayce, a healer of Kentucky. He could put himself in a trance in which he could read the subconscious mind. While in these trances, to help others, he discovered what was causing the disease in his "patients," and how to doctor them. He astounded the medical profession with his amazing discoveries and healings.

COSMIC CONSCIOUSNESS by Dr. Richard Maurice Bucke—This is one of the greatest books that positively states the truth of immortality. It will give any reader a tremendous uplift and stimulation. You will never doubt immortality again.

HEAVEN AND ITS WONDERS AND HELL by Emanuel Swedenborg —This is the most comprehensive and concrete description of life hereafter ever given to mankind: How we enter the next; the spiritual character of our surroundings there; where and how judgment is effected; the universal speech and recreations; these and many other matters are described in detail in Swedenborg's simple, unaffected but compelling words.

These books are available from Master Publications
300 Park Avenue S., New York